GOD GETS EVERYTHING GOD WANTS

KATIE HAYS

WILLIAM B. EERDMANS PUBLISHING COMPANY
GRAND RAPIDS, MICHIGAN

Wm. B. Eerdmans Publishing Co.
4035 Park East Court SE, Grand Rapids, Michigan 49546
www.eerdmans.com

27 26 25 24 23 22 21   1 2 3 4 5 6 7

ISBN 978-0-8028-7856-4

Library of Congress Cataloging-in-Publication Data

Names: Hays, Katie, 1969– author.
Title: God gets everything God wants / Katie Hays.
Description: Grand Rapids, Michigan : William. B. Eerdmans Publishing
    Company, [2021] | Summary: "A rehabilitated theology of hope, inclu-
    sion, and defiance for weary Christians, former Christians, and the
    Christ-curious—especially those who have been excluded from church
    because of who they are and what they (don't) believe"–Provided by
    publisher.
Identifiers: LCCN 2021012161 | ISBN 9780802878564 (hardcover)
Subjects: LCSH: Christian life. | Christianity—Essence, genius, nature.
Classification: LCC BV4501.3 .H3964 2021 | DDC 230—dc23
LC record available at https://lccn.loc.gov/2021012161

Unless otherwise noted, Scripture quotations are from the New Revised
Standard Version Bible, © 1989 National Council of the Churches of Christ
in the United States of America. Used by permission. All rights reserved
worldwide.

for Lance, without whom I wouldn't know or believe anything
(Song of Songs 5:16)

for Lydia & Jack, our boon companions
Here is everything I have to tell you

for Galileo Church, our family's family
I am so glad to be in ministry alongside you

CONTENTS

CONTENTS

Part Four
I Want to Want What God Wants

Part Five
We Want to Want What God Wants

PREFACE

The universal gospel that God gets everything God wants is shaped by location: the people, places, sounds, history, and experiences of Christian community. For me, that location is Galileo Church.*

Look, nobody gets to Galileo Church by accident.

For one thing, we're hard to find. Exit 442A off I-20 on the southeast edge of Fort Worth leads to a tree lot on one side of the interstate. Over on our side there's a Mickey D's, a charity thrift store, a liquor store, a metal-galvanizing plant, and our Big Red Barn. Which is, honestly, not all that big—and more of a rusted, corrugated sheet metal hue.

By the time you show up here, you've probably combed our website obsessively, on high alert for any whiff of the kind of stuff that can bring all your pain back to the surface. You have learned to be exquisitely careful around All Things Christian—church, the Bible, and especially Christians themselves. All that stuff has hurt you. You don't wish to be hurt anymore.

---

* Galileo Christian Church (Disciples of Christ) is a community of belonging in Jesus's name (i.e., a church) on the southeast edge of Fort Worth, Texas, born in 2013 to "seek and shelter spiritual refugees." We're named after the Christian astronomer who scared the church by showing, with his math and his telescope, that we earthlings are not the center of the universe—a view that the church feared would undermine its teaching that human beings are the pinnacle of God's creation. We chose the name in humble recognition that the church itself could use decentering—and because Galileo was devout and kicked out, just like a lot of us. And because we like science.

Photos on our website—of communion, of people singing hymns—make you flinch. You remember the day you stopped pretending you're not gay, or that your cousin or your roommate or your moms aren't gay; or you stopped keeping your mouth shut about the US empire and consumer capitalism and systemic racism and the havoc we keep wreaking on each other and the rest of the world; or you stopped sequestering science from religion in your brain, no longer hoping they'd never meet and have an actual conversation.

And when you stopped doing those things, you slammed into the painful insistence by your church that *you* were the problem: your way of being, your way of thinking, your way of voting, your way of asking pesky questions that unsettle what has long been settled. Maybe they didn't kick you out, not officially—actual excommunication is rare these days, as most (predominantly white, North American, Protestant) churches are desperate to keep everyone and mostly lack the gumption to take a costly stand—but they made it clear that you weren't welcome any longer. Not all of you, anyway. Not 100 percent of your queer or queer-adjacent, skeptical, science-y, socialist-curious self.*

In case it matters to you, can I affirm that your skittish skepticism is a rational response to what you've experienced? Maybe you've already worked this through with your therapist as I have with mine. I hope so. But sometimes it helps to hear again that your decision to walk away from church, if that's what you did, or to simply stop pursuing it when it obviously wasn't that into you, was a healthy one.

But here you are, melting in your car on a hot Sunday afternoon, scooching down in the driver's seat, peering at people making their way through the parking lot, down an asphalt path, and disappearing

---

* I have actually heard, multiple times, of church members being told, "You can still attend worship here, still sign up for certain kinds of service here, still give money here; but you can't have membership status now that we know who you actually are." Yep, for real.

around a corner where there must be a door. A sign chained to a stop sign pointed you to our parking lot.* You simply cannot believe you're contemplating going inside for worship. It's been so long, and you don't understand why you're still drawn to it. "I wish I knew how to quit you," you've said to the church, to God, to the anonymous heavens more times than you can count.** But here you are.

If you came to me today with your confession of how long it's been since you last attended a worship service, and/or how hard it is for you to believe any of this stuff anymore, and/or how impossible it seems to you that God has done anything good to recommend Godself lately—I'd say, "Yeah, and that's on us, the church. It's on the churchy people like me for whom it mostly does work much of the time, we who have made our peace with the church's real failures mostly by ignoring them. We did that to you. We pushed you away, sometimes on purpose, sometimes completely by accident. Whether it was aggression or negligence on our part, you deserved better. I'm so sorry. You don't have to forgive us, but I'd love a chance to make it up to you. No strings. Just . . . come and see."

And what then? If you took me up on it, what would I show you? What could be happening in that sheet metal, not-so-red barn tucked under I-20 that might be worth your time and attention?

I have taken to calling our primary work at Galileo Church "theological rehabilitation." Together we are doing the painstaking work of examining our Christian faith and sorting it out—the good stuff from the harmful stuff, the stuff with integrity from the stuff we simply inherited from family or church or, here in the Bible Belt, the cultural air we're breathing. It's not fast or easy work, and I've come to believe that nobody can really do it on their own. We're

---

* Another sign in the lot warns you to "Trust in the Lord, but DON'T leave your stuff in the car—Matthew 10:16." Look it up; you won't be sorry.

** Say it like Jake Gyllenhaal to Heath Ledger in *Brokeback Mountain*. Say it right out loud. Nobody's listening but God, and God has heard it before.

in it together, trying again to figure out what it means when we make the syllable "God" with our mouths,* or how it forms us to take the name "Christian" for ourselves.

It's risky work, right? To consider again the possibility that God might know exactly who you are and love exactly that about you? To consider again the possibility that the Christian faith might be good for you, helping you to flourish in all the fullness of your gorgeous, sparkly, queer, and/or quirky AF humanity? Maybe that's why we need each other—so none of us bears all the risk alone. Maybe that's what church is supposed to be: people sharing the gamble of faith, daring to hope, taking a chance on love.

Here's what I can't do: I can't say everything that needs to be said to repair all the ways Christian theology has hurt people, including you. That's partly because I can't begin to know all the ways that God and the people of God have disappointed people, including you. And it's partly because I'm not a systematic theologian—that is, I don't have a lot of training or practice in articulating or even aiming at articulating the Whole Truth about God.

But for a long time now I've been listening, and learning, and praying, and studying, and exploring with my church-full of spiritual refugees. We've been exploring together how we might recover ways of expressing Christian faith, faith that is rooted in love and produces real hope. There are ways, I'm telling you, of doing that, so that Christianity is an actual help instead of a hindrance to the flourishing of this world, and the flourishing of you.

What I hope to do in these pages is show you what we've learned over several years of not taking our faith for granted. We've leapt. We've wrestled. We've dreamed and argued and wept and cursed and laughed. We're not saying we've figured everything out, but it's been

---

* A hearty thanks to Rob Bell for reminding us we're not all saying the same thing when we say "God," in *What We Talk About When We Talk About God* (2013).

a damn fine effort, if we do say so ourselves. We've been grateful for the time and space and companionship to work through it. And we're happy now to come alongside you on this path of faith-or-something-like-it. *You didn't get here by accident.* We're really glad you came.

You can tell a lot about an author's theology by how they organize their subject. Do they start with God, or with Jesus? (Nobody starts with the Holy Spirit, bless her heart.) When they talk about people, do they give more pages to Genesis 1 (people are beautiful and bursting with potential) or Genesis 3 (people are broken, deceitful, ashamed)? What's the proportion of time spent with the teachings *of* Jesus versus the teachings *about* Jesus? Where do they mostly locate the activity of God: in the church, or "out there" in the cosmos? Are they more interested in how we should live or in what happens when we die? What do they care about more: what we believe or what we do? Do they tend to imagine human beings relating to God as individuals or as members of the collective human family?

This point about "the organization of the subject" came home to me in a rereading of Douglas John Hall's *Professing the Faith: Christian Theology in a North American Context* (1993). Hall ultimately settled on three main divisions for his systematic work: Theology, Creaturely Being, and Christology. But, he said:

> A . . . finally insoluble limitation must be acknowledged. Like every great story, the story with which Christian theology has to concern itself is characterized by one overarching feature: integrity. . . . Thus the entire practice of separating the parts, of ordering them according to a certain schema, . . . is at some basic level artificial and potentially misleading. Where does Theology leave off and anthropology begin? How does anyone discuss Christology apart from a simultaneous consideration of divinity and creatureliness? In saying this, we are only reiterating the need for modesty. (31–32)

TL;DR: I probably won't get this exactly right, but it's worth a (modest) try.

Modestly speaking, then, here's how we're going to move forward from here:

Introduction

No, this isn't it; you're still in the preface. Hang on a sec.

Part 1: God Gets Everything God Wants

This claim is so basic at Galileo Church that we often abbreviate it: GGEGW. It's a way of talking about God, and God's activity, that is dynamic instead of static. All the prophets know it, and they're itching for the rest of us to catch up.

Part 2: Jesus Is God Getting Everything God Wants

GGEGW has become the lens through which we observe and cheer for Jesus's entire life and ministry, because wherever Jesus is, there God is Getting Everything God Wants. We know what Jesus was obsessed with, and we know why: because he was the Logic of God walking around with skin on. In a hamster ball. Wait for it.

Part 3: When God Doesn't Get Everything God Wants

God insists on partnership with human beings, especially as demonstrated through Jesus's bestowal of the Holy Spirit on his friends and the subsequent not-without-hiccups development of the early church. Sometimes people cooperate with that Spirit and get things amazingly right. And this has become our anthropology: that we are, each and every one of us, grown-ass adults imbued with the Spirit of the living Christ.

Part 4: I Want to Want What God Wants

Here, then, is how to live: by aligning our desires with what God wants, leaning into God's future, finding beautiful what God finds beautiful. Even if it turns out that what God wants most of all is *you*—all of you, and everybody else too.

Part 5: We Want to Want What God Wants

All that stuff I said in part 4? We do that *together*. And that's what makes us a church, subversive and strong and useful in this world God still loves.

Conclusion: What Do You Want?

Well?

THE GOOD AND NECESSARY WORK
OF THEOLOGICAL REHABILITATION

"Come on, come on, come on, you can do it!" the physical therapist urges the person sweating and grunting and gritting their way from one end of the parallel bars to the other. The patient is recovering from a car wreck–induced spinal cord injury, retraining her nervous system and her musculoskeletal system, learning how to walk again like a thirty-year-old toddler. It takes everything she's got to cover three yards or so, and the whole rehab center PT room cheers when she gets to the end.

* * *

The speech therapist exaggerates her own facial movements, lips pushed forward to form "Ooooooo," then stretched wide for "Eeeeeee." The stroke survivor wants more than anything to tell their partner, "I love you, and thank you for sticking with me through all of this." It'll be a while before they can speak all those words with clarity, but progress is coming with several hours of daily rehab.

* * *

The recovering addict confesses to his counselor how terrified he is of drowning in the flood of emotions that have surged now that he's clean and sober. He has miles to go on this journey of learning to feel his own feelings; it won't feel safe for a long time. He'll stay in rehab, doing the work of reconnecting with himself, until everyone on his care team agrees that he can maintain sobriety and manage all the feelings on his own.

* * *

"It's a mess, but it's got good bones," the realtor says to their buyer. "Yeah, I've got some ideas," the buyer says, knocking on walls, already imagining how she can rearrange this square footage to suit her needs. It'll take a year or more working every weekend, but rehabbing an old house—knocking out some walls, tearing out carpet to see what's underneath—sounds like fun. *Bet it's hardwood*, she thinks. *Maybe my girlfriend will want to help.*

Going to Rehab

Some years ago I started talking about my primary work at Galileo Church as "theological rehabilitation." I was drawing on the familiar idea of "rehab," where something old is restored, or something broken is repaired, or something forgotten is relearned, or something neglected is tended to. Rehab is the kind of work that remembers what came before for the sake of what comes next. You're not starting from scratch, building from the ground up; in rehab, you've got material to work with—it just needs rearranging, or recovering, or rebuilding. Above all, it needs *care*; rehab is a slow, care-full process. By paying attention to detail and not getting in a rush, rehab resists doing any further damage. It might take a long time. Do you have the patience for it?

Theological rehabilitation, then, is the slow, care-full work of remembering what we think we know about God, the universe, and everything and figuring out which parts of that are good and true and beautiful so that we can build on what we've got for the sake of new theological understandings. Theological rehabilitation requires an honest assessment of gaps, assumptions, misunderstandings, and propaganda in what we used to think we knew for sure so that we can jettison those in favor of better, richer, more fruitful ways of wondering.

Wonder—that is the primary disposition required for theological rehabilitation, I've learned; and it's the opposite of *certainty*, the opposite of believing that everything we're supposed to understand about God, the universe, and everything has already been settled and is just waiting for our intellectual assent. Wonder, in contrast to certainty, assumes that *unsettledness* is indeed a quality of God and all that God has made. Wonder helps us celebrate the invitation to consider, challenge, discern, and sweat-grunt-grit our way to new understandings, understandings that have built into them the possibility that they, too, will give way to even newer understandings, so long as God remains God and God's people keep wondering.

We've been doing a *lot* of wondering at Galileo Church, as Galileo Church. It's a dialogical process that started mostly by accident, when I started reading the Bible with people who don't feel obligated to give all the expected answers, or capable of generating the "right" answer, or safe in the presence of traditional understandings of All Things Christian.

At Galileo I started reading the Bible (the Bible here imagined as a springboard for theological conversations of all kinds) with spiritual refugees, and preaching sermons for spiritual refugees, and collaborating with spiritual refugees to plan and lead worship, and cooperating with spiritual refugees to build infrastructure for community, and BOOM! I found myself scrambling to escape the easy theological answers, the practiced theological platitudes, of two decades of ministry in traditional church. Now I was surrounded by people who wanted—nay, *demanded*—ways of talking about God, the universe, and everything that were robust enough to counter the twenty-first-century breakdown* and compassionate enough to soothe the hurt that previous theological understandings had inflicted.

What I'm reporting here, then, is a way of talking about God, the universe, and everything that has developed in the context of Galileo Church. Our way of talking is deeply contextual, but isn't everything? It's also *Christian*, and *orthodox*, and above all, *useful* for drawing human hearts near to the heart of Very God.

I suppose I would say** that North American, mostly white,*** progressive Protestant Christianity is widely in need of theological rehabilitation. The pat answers we grew up with are not satisfying the hungry, thirsty refugees who seek shelter with us. Galileo Church doesn't work (insofar as it works!) because of our hipster vibe or our innovative programming (full confession: we don't have much of either of those). It works because the theological rehabilitation we're doing here brings spiritually broken people back to spiritual health. Here, we relearn to walk, speak, and feel *Christianly*, and find ourselves employed as bricks in a rehabbed house, "built together spiritually into a dwelling place for God" (Eph. 2:22).

But before we do any building, some towers have to fall.

The Jenga Tower Comes a-Tumblin' Down

The sin of the conserving church is that they asked us to believe too much.**** Just too many things, too many discrete pieces of Christian doctrine, planed and sanded and varnished through the ages

---

* "21st century breakdown / I once was lost but never was found" (Green Day, "21st Century Breakdown," 2009).

** Is that tentative enough to communicate how hard I'm trying *not* to say that everyone should get on board with every word I'll write in this book?

*** I write from the context of a church that is, indeed, mostly white and culturally white. It's worth noting so that nobody has to guess or assume.

**** The sin of the liberating church is that they made God feckless and boring as hell in the interest of never offending anyone. Fight me.

until they are all the same shape and size, smooth and sturdy, perfect for stacking into a Babel tower of belief. Like Jenga planks in that stacking game, right?

You're given the planks as a kid in Sunday school. Six-day creation, six thousand years ago, something from nothing, plankton and pH and photons and protons springing fully formed from the mind of God: that's one plank. The utter destruction by global flood of Everything That Is a few generations later, with enough species preserved in a big (but really quite small) boat to repopulate the earth in short order: that's plank no. 2.

(*Except for the plants?* you wonder. *How does the olive tree survive the deluge? How now the dandelion and daisy, the grain and grape?* But you don't ask. If you do, they laugh at your delightful, childish curiosity. It's OK, while you're still a kid, to ask that kind of question.)

From those planks you progress through the Bible's pages to ancient Israel's conquest of Palestine (*But isn't it genocidal occupation of someone else's ancestral land? Shh!*); God's wrath manifest in violent defeat of God's own beloveds by foreign armies (*apparently* not *beloved by God*); the birth of a messianic boy to an unmarried girl who consents to impregnation by God's Spirit (*But could she really say no, given the power differential? Isn't that problematic? And where did the Y chromosome come from? God didn't actually . . .* contribute *that, right?*); and so on.

Among the most essential of the blocks is the one that asserts, "Happy are those who obey the Lord; woe to those who don't" (Ps. 1, e.g.). It's undergone way more sanding than the rest in order to fit into the overall structure, because it's so easily and often refuted by experience. Blessings *don't* actually accrue proportionately to our piety and purity, you've noticed. There are plenty of woes for good people, and plenty of good times to be had by some really despicable characters. The older you get, the more you realize there's more than enough indiscriminate and undeserved suffering to go around.

5

"There, there," church people tell you. "God won't give you more than you can handle. Everything happens for a reason. Farther along we'll know all about it." You are not consoled.

In spite of your wonderings and objections, the Jenga tower of faith the conserving church helped you build is smooth and symmetric. Everything has its place; everybody's tower looks pretty much like everyone else's. Conformity is a high good in this way of doing faith. And if all those towers of belief are disturbingly phallic in your imagination, well, that's on-brand too. One of the planks, after all, is patriarchy-as-God-the-Father's-plan.

But you know what's coming, don't you? Either because you've played Jenga, or you've lived this metaphor in real life, or both. At some point, a plank gets pulled out of your tower. You take a high-school biology class and realize that evolution isn't "just" a theory because scientific theories aren't "just" theories at all. In studying world literature you learn that lots of ancient civilizations told stories about globally catastrophic floods and wrathful gods at war.

Then someone spills the secret that Mary's supposed virginity is based on an ancient translation error from Hebrew to Greek, that the prophets figured the Messiah would be born to a "young woman," irrespective of her sexual experience, and that the early church ran with it because extreme misogyny made women's sexuality extremely icky back in the day. So icky that the early church developed a secondary doctrine of "immaculate conception," which is not about Jesus's birth to a virginal Mary but rather *Mary's* birth to "Anne," her made-up mom, who supposedly conceived without sex with her hubby. Then they added on another one, Mary's "perpetual virginity," preserved *perpetually* in a chaste marriage to Joseph. All this patriarchal effort to keep Mary's reputation wholly, erm, *intact*, if you take my meaning.

And of course, there's the whole issue of *you*, the misshapen plank with rough edges that doesn't fit nicely with the others. You're a girl with a disallowed calling to ministry. You're gay, no matter how hard you've prayed to be otherwise. You vote wrong. The prayers and hymns are dry in your mouth. You've heard that "God is love," but you can't reconcile that with the church's teaching that God actually hates certain people exactly as much as we do.[*] You fight to keep the block of yourself built into the tower, but you feel yourself slipping.

One Jenga plank slides out; the tower wobbles but keeps standing. Another, then another, discredited and discarded doctrines set aside, out of view, while you keep concentrating on keeping the tower together. And then, one too many planks gets pulled, and in the next strong breeze, *boom!* The tower comes a-tumblin' down.

And there you sit, dazed and probably (spiritually) concussed, in the rubble of what used to be your faith. Whether it happened over protracted years or in a short season, it's a horrible place to end up. The tower was your anchor, your ebenezer.[**] Now what will you do? Now who will you be?

Considered Faith; or, Cherish the Atheists

Rummaging through the planks to find what's still usable for the rebuilding of a smaller but sturdier tower is the first postcrash impulse of many Christians. (Or people-formerly-known-as-Christians? When the tower falls, are you still Christian? I'm not asking; you're asking.) Some are lucky enough to salvage a bit of their own identity as a spiritual person in the care of a Spiritual Being. They go, like, "I'm spiritual but not religious, in touch with my existence as more than the sum total of instinct and intellect,

---

[*] On the idiocy of imagining God hating all the same people we do, see Anne Lamott's *Traveling Mercies: Some Thoughts on Faith* (1999).

[**] You know, "Eben-Ezer," "Stone of Help," from 1 Samuel 4–7, where the priest Samuel sets up a stone to commemorate the Israelites' defeat of the Philistines after a lot of drama involving the ark of the covenant and a God-arranged pestilence of hemorrhoids. Yep, for real, that's in there.

but not needful of religious infrastructure or tradition to sustain my connection with the Universe, or the universe's God, whichever." Spiritual But Not Religious can be lonely, I've learned from some of my favorite SBNRs. But SBNR is *something*, which is so much better than *nothing*.

Nothing is miserable to those who once believed. I know a jillion of them, fundagelicals who stumbled away from the rubble of their faith tower with empty hands, having realized that their belief in God was predicated entirely on their belief in all that other stuff, all the accretions of Sunday school stories and ecclesial tradition and family loyalty, such that when those things are gone, there's nothing left. Just *a*-theism, the *not*-God-ness of this planet and our lives on it. You would not believe how many former believers, those heartbroken atheists, occupy the Big Red Barn on any given Sunday night.

Or maybe you would. I was the guest preacher at a traditional, liberating Protestant church one Sunday morning. The sermon included a riff on atheism as a rational response to the lack of evidence for God's presence and power in the world (more homiletically nuanced than that, of course). I said, "If you're sitting here thinking I must be confused about where we are because there are no atheists in church, think again. Atheism is alive and well in the pews of contemporary Christianity, and it produces a profound ache of the heart that churches must make room for, and treat gently, with a great deal of compassion and grace." And a woman in the choir loft blurted out a very loud, "YOU KNOW IT!," which I took to be her own confession of unbelief. From, I reiterate, the choir loft.

I cherish the atheists in my life and in my church. I love preaching to atheists, or people who take none of what they used to believe for granted anymore. They come with me, in my mind's eye, when I burrow into scripture each week. They keep me tethered to the real experience of God's absence and the real experience of life's cruelties. They are largely responsible for the ways I've developed of talking about God, ways that are faithful and Christian but not pretending to a certainty I cannot support.

Indeed, I have come to cherish the atheism that has taken up residence in one chamber of my very own heart. Not because I don't believe in God—but because I have taken very seriously the *possibility* of not believing in God.* My tower crashed a long time ago; I walked away from the rubble with empty hands; I returned to the wreckage to sift through it again; I grieved its loss deeply and finally came to some measure of peace with its collapse. Whatever faith I have now, I like to say, kisses doubt squarely on the mouth every morning of the world.

But listen, I will tell you a parable: Rummaging through the debris of my fallen tower of faith, I found a couple of nuggets that shone like gold. They had been built into the tower, disguised as doctrine, unrecognizable as liberating truth. But now, from the wreckage, they winked at me by the light of day. They wanted to be found. I picked them up, dusted them off, and ate them. Swallowed them whole.

And there they sit to this day, somewhere in the middle of me, thrumming with possibility.

Thrum.

Thrum.

Thrum.

---

* Concerning the spectrum that ranges from "considered faith" to "considered atheism," and how that spectrum can be bent into a circle so that considered faith and considered atheism meet each other, more like helpful friends than opposing sides, see *Patience with God: The Story of Zacchaeus Continuing in Us* by Tomáš Halík (2009). FWIW, Halík locates "certainty" on the opposite side of the circle, 180 degrees away from either considered faith or considered atheism.

PART ONE

GOD GETS EVERYTHING GOD WANTS

1

ONLY TWO STORIES (OK, ONLY ONE)

What if, instead of a Babel tower of symmetric, stacking blocks, we pictured faith like a pattern of concentric circles? Like a dartboard, or—better, for the absence of sharp, spiky projectiles—like the ripples that disturb the water around a pebble you just plunked into a pond?* In the middle of all the rings, a hot, molten core like the center of the earth, glowing and gorgeous. In the middle of me, the glowing golden nuggets I dug from the rubble of my faith and swallowed. (Mixing metaphors, I know. But I trust you, dear reader, to be nimble and forgiving.) Moving out from the center, rings that are further and further away are less and less connected to that core.

Then, concerning what we believe or trust or fear or hope with respect to God, the universe, and everything, we could locate a very small set of Very Important Things in the hot, molten core. Moving out from the core, there would be possibilities for faith, things to believe in or not. But the further away from the center you got, the less likely you'd be to, you know, argue the point.**

---

* This visual of concentric circles, and the foundation for so much of this section, were articulated best, for me, in Walter Brueggemann's *The Bible Makes Sense*, rev. ed. (2003). What I'm doing here isn't exactly what Brueggemann was doing in *TBMS*, but it definitely grows out of my reading of that book with an early Galileo study group. I'd be silly not to say how grateful I am for his inspired and inspiring theological imagination.

** Some friendly fundagelicals use this idea to decide who they can be "in fellowship" with. They call the center of all the circles "salvation issues," and don't

I happen to think when people come to Galileo Church they deserve to know what's in my hot, molten core. Like, what do I believe so hard that I believe it in my bones? Having confessed that I believe a lot less than I used to (I mean, quantitatively fewer pieces of Christian doctrine than I used to), having told you that my own tower of faith collapsed a long time ago, you should be asking me, as I would ask you: What is left? What invaluable pieces were exposed when the tower toppled, that you excavated and hung on to? *What is the content of this gospel you keep preaching, anyway?*

Thanks for asking!

To move toward my answer to that question, we have to take another look at The Greatest Story Ever Told—aka the Bible.

God versus Pretenders: God Wins! (Part One)

What if I told you there's really only one narrative in the whole Bible? Only one main character, only one main plotline? And every story our ancestors told, every commandment they chiseled into stone or had written on their hearts, every mile that Jesus and his followers trudged through Galilee and Jerusalem and to the ends of the earth, every bit of it was in support of one grand thesis? One Big Idea?*

---

want to fight about stuff that's far from the heart of their faith. I applaud this impulse, though I wouldn't label my center "salvation issues," for reasons that should become apparent later; and I've seen that it's way too easy to pack that center circle, reconstructing a Jenga tower up and out of the placid pond ripples, so that just about everything is once again "essential" to being on God's right side.

* My favorite exposition of the "one big story, one big idea" theme is by Bryan Stone in *Evangelism After Christendom: The Theology and Practice of Christian Witness* (2006). In Stone's part 2, "The Story of the People of God," he discusses the three main narratives of the Bible: (1) God's commitment to chosen Israel; (2) Jesus's commitment to the reign of God; and (3) the early church's commitment to the story of Jesus. Then he shows that these three stories cooperate to

The main character, the Protagonist, is God. The plotline is, God wins. The thesis, the One Big Idea, is *God Gets Everything God Wants.*

Let me show you what I mean.

The story begins, as all good stories do, "Once upon a time." Or, "In the beginning"—same difference. And there follows, in Genesis, the establishment of setting ("the heavens and the earth") and the introduction of our Protagonist (God), along with a cast of supporting characters (all of us, all of creation). Rather quickly in the telling, it's established that the character called God is in charge of the whole enchilada—God made it, God set it in motion, God knows how it's all supposed to work, and God thinks it's terrific.

But it's also the case, from very early in the story, that God's in-chargeness is disputed. The world might indeed belong to God and sing God's name, but God is not the kind of god who micromanages, so there are all kinds of chances for things to go wrong—i.e., against the grain of what God wants for and from God's world. We'll come back to that later.

For now, we can jump ahead just a little ways, to Exodus, and find God in a good ol'-fashioned turf war with a powerful antagonist called Pharaoh. Pharaoh pretty much believes that the world is *his* hamburger, as all empire builders are inclined to believe; and so he believes he can take whatever he wants from it, including a labor force of enslaved people to build all his cool stuff. To mark his territory, as it were.

---

reveal a biblical "social imaginary" in which (1) God offers shalom to oppressed Israel; (2) Jesus's ministry offers hope to the marginalized; and (3) the apostolic witness identifies Jesus *with* the marginalized in his death, so that his resurrection is God's vindication of all who suffer for righteousness' sake. The point is: all three stories *are the same story,* funding the same social imaginary in which God acts specifically and deliberately on behalf of what (who) is small, powerless, and #losing. The Bible keeps saying, again and again, that *this is the way the world works, because this is who God is.*

But our guy* God, as it turns out, has a keen ear for suffering (Exod. 2:23–25). The enslaved people groan because of all they've endured for so long (because some pain is only expressible in proto-linguistic sounds; because that's how chronic, generational trauma and suffering *changes* people; and because they've long since forgotten that their ancestors were tight with the God of the cosmos). And God goes, "Hey, this is not how my world is supposed to work!" And God gets busy on a plan to liberate the enslaved people from Pharaoh—not just Pharaoh the man but Pharaoh the *system*, Pharaoh the *mindset*, the *way things work* when Pharaoh is in charge.

God throws down to Pharaoh: "Let my people go." And Pharaoh's like, "Nuh-uh, those are *my* people. You can't have 'em." And now they're wrestling, and Pharaoh's losing, and the way this story goes, God will stop at nothing to show Pharaoh who's the boss. God is willing to work it out so that nobody gets hurt, but Pharaoh's not, and if violence is the only rule Pharaoh respects, it's completely within God's power to be violent in order to establish that the stuff God has made, including people, can't be dominated by any pretenders to the cosmic throne.

End result: *God gets what God wants.* The liberated people now known as "the people of God," or "God's people," spend the rest of Exodus, Leviticus, Numbers, and Deuteronomy getting used to a world where God is in charge. They have things to learn, such as:

> how to rest every seventh day, trusting that they don't have to work and worry 100 percent of the time. In God's economy (distinct from Pharaoh's economy) rest is built into the calendar (for all humans, work animals, and even the dirt) to reinforce the memory that everything they have comes from God anyway, by the power of God's own intervention and gift, not by the sweat of their own brow, as before.

---

* In no way do I assert that God is a "guy," as in, a male. But come on, guys. I'm tryna tell a story here.

> how to open their clenched fists and let go, giving up some of their best stuff to God and to each other, in trust that God's provision is abundant and they can therefore afford to be generous.
> how to govern themselves cooperatively, with rules that protect the vulnerable and restrain the powerful, drawing individual persons into a collective identity as a people.
> how to trust that what God wants is ultimately good for them, even when they don't have a road map for their journey and can't see very far ahead and thus can't pretend to control their own destiny.

Letting God be God is really hard, as it turns out, and requires a lot of very specific instructions and tons of practice, including any number of mistakes. But all those instructions, all that practice, and all those mistakes are in support of the One Big Idea in the Bible: *God gets everything God wants.*

The careful reader will notice that the Hebrew Bible* basically recapitulates this whole story—the liberation of the small, disempowered Israelite tribes and their subsequent formation into a people made strong by being in covenant with the God of the universe—*over and over and over again.* Sometimes it's really obvious, like in Deuteronomy 6:20–25, where the Israelites are asked to tell the story of their ancestors' liberation from Egypt forever, to their kids and their kids' kids and so on. Or like in Ezra 6:19–22, where after a jillion generations and lots of geopolitical drama the remnant of Israelites returning again to their beloved Jerusalem reintroduces the annual celebration of Passover to commemorate God's sound defeat of Pharaoh many hundreds of years ago as if it just happened.

---

* I used to call it the "Old Testament," but for Jews then and now, including Jesus himself, it was/is the *whole* Bible, and it was written (mostly) in Hebrew. It's a sign of respect for the integrity of the collection, and for the people for whom it is the Bible, to differentiate it from Christian scripture by calling it "the Hebrew Bible."

Sometimes the recapitulation of Exodus is more subtle, as when biblical prophets and poets name God the "Redeemer," because "redeeming" is the action word for rescuing someone from enslavement or captivity. Or they'll go completely metaphorical, drawing attention to God's "mighty hand and outstretched arm," the body parts by which God was said to have bested Pharaoh (Deut. 4:34, 2 Chron. 6:32, Ps. 89:13, Jer. 21:5 . . . we could go on and on).

The point is: no matter what part of the Hebrew Bible you're reading, you're basically reading the story of Exodus again and again. God takes on a pretender to God's throne; God rescues a small, oppressed people; God forms the liberated little ones into God's people; God promises to love and take care of them forever; God's feelings get super hurt when they reject God's forever love and care. "The Exodus is how we know who God is," the Hebrew Bible says. "The Exodus is how we know who God will always be."

God versus Pretenders: God Wins! (Part Two)

"OK," you might be saying now. "OK, I checked it out and there is sure 'nuff a lot of Exodus in the Hebrew Bible. Makes sense. But what about the New Testament? That's not about Exodus. That's about Jesus, obviously. Right?"

Exactly right: the Christian scriptures introduce us to Jesus—who, by the way, himself celebrated Passover, as one of the descendants of those faithful Israelites who told the Exodus story again and again and again. And in a while I'll have lots more to say about Jesus's ministry as reported in the Gospels. But for this moment, let's stay with the One Big Idea: that *God gets everything God wants*, even when it means doing combat with pretenders to God's throne.

Jesus of Nazareth was born in the region of Galilee, one of thousands of provinces that the Roman Empire had swallowed up in its attempt to rule the world. His entire life was lived under occupation by an army under Caesar's command, an army with orders to enforce Caesar's ownership and bankroll Caesar's expansion by oppressive taxation that kept people working relentlessly. It wasn't Pharaoh's enslavement, exactly, but it was close.

And it was Roman imperial law that could not tolerate anyone who threatened or subverted Caesar's authority. It was under Roman imperial law that anyone who competed with Caesar for the loyalty of his subjects could be executed. It was the Roman imperial judicial system, represented in a sham trial with perjured witnesses (Mark 15:3-4), that found Jesus guilty, sentenced him to death, and executed him. Yep, there was an entanglement there with religious authorities who themselves felt threatened by stuff Jesus said and did, but it was a Roman imperial court that decided his fate and a Roman imperial military police force that carried out his sentence.

When his followers told the story later they would insist that the Roman Empire and its Caesar were too puny to be named as the perpetrators of Jesus's death. They would say it was Death Itself what done it—that the Enemy Death carried Jesus into captivity, intending to permanently enslave him in nonexistence (Acts 2:24, Rom. 6:9). The Romans simply acted as Death's unwitting proxy. At the most basic level, one way to say why Jesus had to die is that *everybody dies*—because Death has a hold on humanity, like a Pharaoh or a Caesar, pretending that it can do what it wants, take what it wants, because it can't be beat.

But listen, don't ever tell God that you can't be beat. Don't ever pretend that the world is your hamburger. Because God will take that challenge, and God will whoop your ass. Pharaoh, Caesar, even Death itself, and the systems that afford them their illegitimate power—God goes up against all of them and God declares victory. That's how this story *always* goes, according to the Bible.

Like, in the case of Jesus and his captivity to Death, his lifeless body lying in a cold tomb over the weekend, waiting for someone to take care of it—God takes one look at that, and God says, "Nope." And God calf-ropes Death. Just in case you're not from Texas: God (on horseback, of course) lassos Death around the neck, jumps down from the horse, flips Death over on its back, ties three of Death's legs together, and won't let go until Death surrenders and gives back what Death stole from God. And that, guys and gals and nonbinary pals, is what we call *resurrection*.

And it can be argued—I'm arguing!—that the Christian scriptures recapitulate the resurrection of Jesus *over and over and over again*. Even before his death, whenever Jesus walks on water or multiplies food or heals sick bodies or restores family relationships, the Gospels foreshadow his resurrection, hinting broadly that he simply isn't bound by the laws of the natural universe the way the rest of us are. When the early church turned an annual Passover feast into a far more frequent celebration of eating and drinking at the eucharistic meal, they said they were remembering Jesus's death "until he comes" (1 Cor. 11:26). Remembering that he died, that is, but didn't stay dead! Alleluia!

When they remembered how he was in life and encouraged each other to be more like that, more like Jesus, no matter the cost or consequence, because after all, we know God's got our back, just like God had his back . . . that's resurrection!

All of which is to say: *God gets everything God wants*. Exodus and resurrection are, in a sense, the same plotline with different details. Everything belongs to God; God has a way God wants all this to go; someone else dares to compete with God for control of the show; God's mighty hand and outstretched arm do their thing; and God wins. Pharaoh, Caesar, Death—they do not stand a snowball's chance in the hell I no longer believe in (more on that later). *God gets everything God wants*. Thanks be to God!

2

THE ARC OF THE MORAL UNIVERSE

When I was growing up, it was the one about Dad and Mom driving from New York to their family-of-origin homes in Texas (hers) and New Mexico (his) before they were married, before they were "Dad" and "Mom," so they could meet each other's families; and on that endless car trip they decided to get married while they were home, and their families were mostly happy but also kind of miffed to have to plan a wedding on the fly.

For my kids, it's probably the one about that time we (my spouse and me, before we were "Mom and Dad") woke up in our third-story New Haven apartment to the sound of breaking glass down below and, looking out the window, saw the thief breaking into our car; but he didn't steal the car, he just stole the quarters we were saving for the laundromat, and we were super sad, because those quarters were important to our quality of life.

Or my insistence, especially in those moments when my actual physicality doesn't match my aspirational physicality (i.e., I get winded on a family hike), that "I used to be a runner," which I think should count somehow in my kids' assessment of me even though I only ever managed one 10K when both kids were babies, and it was the one sponsored by Entenmann's Bakery on Long Island where everybody got free donuts at the end.

We all recognize the phenomenon, right? That lots of us, as we age, tell the same stories repeatedly, wistful for a past in which we were happier, peppier, whatever-er. It's called nostalgia, a longing for the past when things were better than they are now, at least in our imaginations.

Hear me now: it's important to recognize that that's *not* what the Hebrew Bible or the Christian scriptures are doing when they recapitulate the Exodus and Jesus's resurrection again and again. When they relay the One Big Idea that *God Gets Everything God Wants*, it's not past tense—"Once upon a time, God *got* everything God *wanted*, and boy, wasn't that something?" The scriptures are not nostalgic for a time that has passed away.

Rather, our ancestors in faith assert by their remembrances a faith claim: *Because* we have experienced God having gotten what God wanted in the past, *because* we know God defeated powerful foes along the way to get it, we are also certain that, in this moment and henceforth evermore, God *is getting* and *will get* everything God wants. God *gets* everything God wants: then, now, and forever.

The fancy (and useful) phrase for this is *eschatological faith.* "Eschatology" is the study of "last things"—that is to say, the final destiny of the universe and everything in it. Eschatological faith is the belief that this whole rodeo is directional, history is headed somewhere, the universe has a destiny, the future will culminate in . . . something. According to our ancestors in faith, that "something" is whatever God wants it to be. Because *God, ultimately, gets everything God wants.* (Am I repeating that idea enough? Should I say it more? Note to self: say it more.)

The Hebrew Bible Prophets Saw It

When the biblical prophets proclaimed God's badassery, they said that everybody better shape up, and people with money and power better stop stepping on people without money and power, and kings who bragged that theirs was the biggest (army, of course!) were in for a big surprise, and those who suffered should hang on just a lit-

tle while longer for the relief they badly needed. Help/consolation/
reckoning/judgment is coming, the prophets said. And they made
those claims based on the One Big Idea that God *gets* (has gotten, is
getting, will get) everything God wants.

The biblical prophets had lots to say about things gone horribly
wrong, painfully against-the-God-grain in God's beloved world.
Lots of things would need to be undone, they said—corrupt kings and
kingdoms toppled, religious fraud rooted out, the perils of building
wealth on the backs of the poor exposed—so that God could rebuild the
world according to God's own desires. "You have to break a lot of eggs
to make an omelet," the prophets prophesied. And for most of them
the egg breaking was happening all around them as they spoke. They
weren't so much divining the future as describing the present reality
and interpreting the social, political, and religious chaos as God's own
initiative, God's insistence on getting what God wanted.

But most of the Hebrew Bible prophets also talked about something they had not seen with their literal eyeballs. They had visions
of the ultimate destiny of the whole wide world. They painted as-
tonishing, captivating word pictures of what it could look like, not
now but someday, when God gets everything God wants, eschatologically speaking.* For example:

> In days to come
> the mountain of the LORD's house
> shall be established as the highest of the mountains,
> and shall be raised up above the hills.
> Peoples shall stream to it,
> and many nations shall come and say:

---

* Rabbi Lauren Holtzblatt said at Justice Ruth Bader Ginsberg's memorial service on September 23, 2020, "To be able to see beyond the world you are in, to
imagine that something could be different—that is the job of a prophet. And
it is the rare prophet who not only imagines a new world but also makes that
new world a reality in her lifetime." Amen.

"Come, let us go up to the mountain of the LORD,
    to the house of the God of Jacob;
that [God]* may teach us [God's] ways
    and that we may walk in [God's] paths."
For out of Zion shall go forth instruction,
    and the word of the LORD from Jerusalem.
[God] shall judge between many peoples,
    and shall arbitrate between strong nations far
        away;
they shall beat their swords into plowshares,
    and their spears into pruning hooks;
nation shall not lift up sword against nation,
    neither shall they learn war any more;
but they shall all sit under their own vines
and under their own fig trees,
    and no one shall make them afraid;**
    for the mouth of the LORD of hosts has spoken.
        (Mic. 4:1–4)

Or this one:

On this mountain the LORD of hosts will make for all
      peoples
    a feast of rich food, a feast of well-aged wines,
    of rich food filled with marrow, of well-aged wines
      strained clear.

---

*   Scripture quotations throughout this book are from the New Revised Standard Version, but it's the practice at Galileo Church to replace gendered pronouns for the Deity. Those replacements are in brackets.

**   Did you know that George Washington cited Micah 4:4 almost fifty times in his correspondence? Lin-Manuel Miranda did. It was President Washington's own personal eschatological vision for retirement, and for his fellow citizens. The more you know!

> And [God] will destroy on this mountain
>> the shroud that is cast over all peoples,
>> the sheet that is spread over all nations;
>> [God] will swallow up death forever.
> Then the Lord GOD will wipe away the tears from
>> all faces,
>> and the disgrace of [God's] people [God] will take
>>> away from all the earth,
>> for the LORD has spoken.
> It will be said on that day,
> Lo, this is our God; we have waited for [God], so that
>> [God] might save us.
>> This is the LORD for whom we have waited;
>> let us be glad and rejoice in [God's] salvation.
>> (Isa. 25:6-9)

There are many more, but perhaps these suffice for now. Based on these passages, what could we say it looks like when God ultimately gets everything God wants? After all the egg breaking, what delectable, divine omelet is on the cosmic breakfast plate?

To the prophet Micah, it looks like . . . the people of the world coming together to hear and follow God's instructions about the way the world is supposed to work . . . the end of warfare, as people learn from God to repurpose the weaponry we have amassed and used to assert power and ownership, making weapons into tools for farming and caring for the land together . . . the fair distribution of land to all, so that each can produce what is needed for a bountiful, secure life . . . and the absence of fear or defensiveness or protectionism, as everyone already has enough.

To the prophet Isaiah, it looks like . . . a ginormous party that everyone is invited to, with food so rich it makes your teeth ache and wine so fine the guests are intoxicated by its taste alone . . . the destruction of Death once and for all, when God selects Death as

25

God's own appetizer, bites its head off and "swallows [it] up" . . . the subsequent soothing of all sadness and the release from all shame . . . and the raucous whoop by those whose long wait for this day has finally been vindicated.

These are Big Pictures, cosmic reorderings, totalizing visions sent from the mind of God to the minds of the prophets so they could see and show the possibilities for this world. "The world could work like this," Micah and Isaiah and their colleagues said; "and someday it will, just you wait."

New Testament Prophets Saw It

In the New Testament, too, there are reports of and from God's prophets, the ones who are gifted with incredibly long-distance vision, the ones who peer from this present (painful) moment into God's yearned-for future and report back to everyone else what they have seen. In the Gospels, both John the Baptist and Jesus himself function as prophets, disclosing what they've been shown (or learned to see?) to anybody who will listen.

I especially love the way Luke's Gospel introduces John the Baptist, locating John's life work with political and religious specificity, as if to say, "This is the world he lived in, but there's a whole 'nother world he could see." Like this:

> In the fifteenth year of the reign of Emperor Tiberius, when Pontius Pilate was governor of Judea, and Herod was ruler of Galilee, and his brother Philip ruler of the region of Ituraea and Trachonitis, and Lysanias ruler of Abilene, during the high priesthood of Annas and Caiaphas, the word of God came to John son of Zechariah in the wilderness. He went into all the region around the Jordan, proclaiming a baptism of repentance for the forgiveness of sins, as it is written in the book of the words of the prophet Isaiah,

"The voice of one crying out in the wilderness:
   'Prepare the way of the Lord,
     make his paths straight.
   Every valley shall be filled,
     and every mountain and hill shall be made low,
   and the crooked shall be made straight,
     and the rough ways made smooth;
   and all flesh shall see the salvation of God.'"
        (Luke 3:1-6, quoting Isa. 40:3-4)

Luke saw John the Baptist fulfilling a role foreseen by the prophetic granddaddy Isaiah, bringing to life a little piece of Isaiah's eschatological vision. Preparation for the Messiah's coming would require leveling the human playing field by lowering mountains and raising valleys (metaphorically, though, yeah? not literally bulldozing the landscape, right? more on that later), so that everybody (all flesh!) could have an equal shot at eyeballing God's work on their behalf. Because "the salvation of God" was coming, John ranted from his camp on the outskirts of civilization. God was just about to get everything God wants, and everybody better be ready when it happened.

Jesus spoke often of what it would look like when God gets everything God wants, something we'll pick up in the next chapter. But for now, just this sample:

Once more Jesus spoke to them in parables, saying: "The kingdom of heaven may be compared to a king who gave a wedding banquet for his son. He sent his slaves* to call those who had

* If we were reading this passage together in worship at Galileo Church, we would pause here to acknowledge how problematic and painful it is to hear the language of enslavement in Jesus's mouth. We wouldn't be able to fix it on the fly, but we would pause. You could pause here, too, in your reading. It's not enough, but it might be better than nothing.

been invited to the wedding banquet, but they would not come. Again he sent other slaves, saying, 'Tell those who have been invited: Look, I have prepared my dinner, my oxen and my fat calves have been slaughtered, and everything is ready; come to the wedding banquet.' But they made light of it and went away, one to his farm, another to his business, while the rest seized his slaves, mistreated them, and killed them. The king was enraged. He sent his troops, destroyed those murderers, and burned their city. Then he said to his slaves, 'The wedding is ready, but those invited were not worthy. Go therefore into the main streets, and invite everyone you find to the wedding banquet.' Those slaves went out into the streets and gathered all whom they found, both good and bad; so the wedding hall was filled with guests." (Matt. 22:1–10)

He, too, sounds like Isaiah, imagining a fantastic dinner party with a beautifully appointed table and enough seats for everyone who comes. I don't know how much barbecue you get out of oxen (plural!) and fat calves, but it's plenty; all the prophets concur that God doesn't scrimp on the eschatological refreshments. In Jesus's vision, ungrateful guests would be, *ahem*, uninvited; but absolutely everyone else who could be pulled from their pressing business would be eagerly welcome. "Everyone" here includes, explicitly, "both good and bad" (v. 10), as if God's guest list is not exactly exclusive. God just really likes company.

OK, one more. Remember how I said the Bible starts out like all good stories do, with "Once upon a time" (Gen. 1:1)? Well, stories that start that way have to end with "And they all lived happily ever after." Which the Bible does, with John the Apostle's vision in the New Testament book called Revelation. There's a whole lotta demolition in there, in the tradition of the Hebrew Bible prophets who knew you can't start a kitchen reno till you tear out the old cabinets and flooring. No cooking for weeks, the coffee pot plugged in on the bathroom counter—it's miserable. But then one day there's the brand spanking new kitchen you've waited so long for:

> Then I saw a new heaven and a new earth; for the first heaven and the first earth had passed away, and the sea was no more. And I saw the holy city, the new Jerusalem, coming down out of heaven from God, prepared as a bride adorned for her husband. And I heard a loud voice from the throne saying,
>
> > "See, the home of God is among mortals.
> > [God] will dwell with them;
> > they will be [God's] peoples,
> > and [God's own self] will be with them;
> > [God] will wipe every tear from their eyes.
> > Death will be no more;
> > mourning and crying and pain will be no more,
> > for the first things have passed away."
>
> . . . Then the angel showed me the river of the water of life, bright as crystal, flowing from the throne of God and of the Lamb through the middle of the street of the city. On either side of the river is the tree of life with its twelve kinds of fruit, producing its fruit each month; and the leaves of the tree are for the healing of the nations. Nothing accursed will be found there any more. But the throne of God and of the Lamb will be in it, and [God's] servants will worship; they will see [God's] face, and [God's] name will be on their foreheads. And there will be no more night; they need no light of lamp or sun, for the Lord God will be their light, and they will reign forever and ever. (Rev. 21:1–4; 22:1–5)

There's a lot going on here, yeah? John the Revelator describes a homecoming parade celebrating God's long-awaited return to the company of creation and beloved humanity. He reports matter-of-factly the destruction of Death and all the pain that Death has caused. He points out the botanical source of reconciliation for warring nations and for the healing of the battered, broken world. He reveals God's happy sharing of God's power with all God's beloveds. John's revelation adds to the layers of lusciousness that all the biblical prophets saw and longed for, recognizing that it was still a ways off, over the distant horizon of God's "someday."

So, to recap: There is One Big Idea underlying the biblical prophets' visions of what comes next (like, soon) and what comes someday. When the Bible speaks repeatedly of something that has happened in the past (exodus, resurrection), it's not being nostalgic for a lovely past we should wish to return to. And when the Bible speaks longingly of something that hasn't happened yet, it's not wishful thinking about a dreamy future where we get all the ice cream we want. (Nor all the choral singing or all the sexual pleasure or all the whatever you think might make you happy forever. That's a heaven I don't believe in anymore. Because it's not about what *you* want, right? It's about GGEGW.)

Instead, the past and the future are tied together, the Bible says, by the singular Protagonist of this singular story. Because God has gotten what God wants (past), God can/will get what God wants (future). History is going somewhere, toward a future of God's own imagining, and maybe you are already getting the idea that the future of God's own imagining has something to say about the present we are living through right this minute.

Contemporary Prophets See It

Visions of the cosmic future (relentlessly tied to our ancestral past) when God gets everything God wants (because God has gotten what God wants) did not stop with the closure of the Bible. Prophets in every age have been able to see it, and they've been gracious to show the rest of us what they've seen. Moreover, their visions have fueled their own sense of the urgency of now in ministry, in governance, in economics, in advocacy, in life, and have inspired many to follow in their footsteps. Here's a sample:

> The Rev. Dr. Martin Luther King Jr. took a long view of the civil rights movement in a 1968 sermon at Washington National Cathedral, drawing on the work of abolitionist Unitarian minister Rev. Theodore Parker: "We shall overcome because the arc of the moral universe is long, but it bends toward justice," King said. History and human existence are not static, he meant; there is a goal, a destination, for all of humanity and all the cosmos together. That destiny he called "justice," which Dr. Cornel West, professor at Union Theological Seminary, defines as "what love looks like in public." Both Drs. King and West would agree: the eschatological recognition that justice for all people is God's intention for the future means we can (and had better!) respond to that recognition by advancing justice for all people *now*.

> Bishop Desmond Tutu riffed on MLK's 1963 "I Have a Dream" speech for his book *God Has a Dream* (2004). He writes,

> God says to you, "I have a dream. . . . It is a dream of a world whose ugliness and squalor and poverty, its war and hostility, its greed and harsh competitiveness, its alienation and disharmony are changed into their glorious counterparts. When there will be more laughter, joy, and peace, where there will be justice and goodness and compassion and love and caring and sharing. I have a dream that my children will know that they are members of one family, the human family, God's family, my family." (19–20)

But don't think for a minute Bishop Tutu imagined that God's vision should wait for divine fulfillment in the sweet by-and-by. He was awarded the Nobel Peace Prize in 1984 for his leadership in South Africa's transition from apartheid to majority rule, because his eschatological vision gave him work to do *now*.

> Dominican priest Gustavo Gutiérrez, one of the founders of liberation theology in the twentieth century, didn't claim to see every detail of God's coming future. He was skeptical of humans' attempts to describe a sociopolitical utopia and published his own revised visions as he learned more about the human family all around him. But he argued strenuously for the "non-necessity of the present order" (a delicious phrase! chew on that awhile!), meaning anything that got in God's way would disintegrate eventually anyway. From this eschatological conviction he preached the dismantling of oppressive systems *now* based on his understanding of God's dream for the world.

There have been, and still are, so many more. But these are sufficient to demonstrate that the church has always had prophetic visionaries who peer into the future and see a time coming when all of creation, everything that is, will be re-formed into the world God always had in mind. Some egg breaking, some serious demolition of the "present order," might be required along the way, but both the ancient and not-so-ancient prophets know this for sure: *God gets everything God wants*, then, now, and forever.

PART TWO

JESUS IS GOD GETTING EVERYTHING GOD WANTS

3

THE EMBODIED LOGIC OF GOD

Before we get too much further I should say, as clearly as I can, that Jesus is not, for me, just another one of the prophets with extraordinary eschatological vision. Galileo Church is *Christian*, meaning that we confess our allegiance to the dark-skinned Palestinian Jew named Jesus who came from Nazareth as our Christ, our brother, our friend, our teacher, our exemplar, our savior, our Lord.* I believe that Jesus is the fullest expression of God-among-us that the world has known.

That's not to say there are not, have not been, other expressions of God-among-us. I celebrate the faith of Muslim and Jewish friends (and strangers), as I believe God has made Godself known among them. I am curious about and appreciative of all religious faiths and

---

* I pay attention to those for whom "Lord" is a problematic title because it connotes a class system in which "lords" are landowners, sometimes people-enslavers, definitely socially dominant in a money-and-status kind of way. I'm stubbornly hopeful that Jesus-as-Lord can rehabilitate our own perverted ideas of class, wealth, and power, however. Especially because Jesus-as-*crucified*-Lord, with his insistence on coming-to-serve-not-to-be-served, is a potent antidote to our ideas about striving for status. I wouldn't, however, insist that the word-for-word confession "Jesus is Lord" is in the hot, molten core of my faith. I think there are other ways to express devotion and loyalty to him, and I think he's OK with that—as long as we're not calling anybody else "Lord." Or behaving as willing subjects to any other system of lordship, seductive as they may be. He really doesn't like that, I've heard.

spiritual practices and philosophical ponderings that seek to connect the human spirit to the world we can see and to worlds we cannot.

I am hyperaware that my own Christian identity was, in the first place, granted me by virtue of being born into a Christian household. As I heard a rabbi say once, "I am Jewish because I was dandled on a Jewish knee." It's a humble admission that one's faith is, in large part, dependent on where and when and to whom one was born. But over time, as I came to understand that Christian discipleship is a swirl of inheritance and decision and habit and hope, I found that, with practice, I got better at the decision part; and, over time, decisions became habit; and, through the years, even what I hope for has been refined and reformed; and, consequently, I am more Christian today than I was when I was born, or when I was young, or yesterday.

Listen, I will tell you a parable. My spouse and I graduated from divinity school and moved to Birmingham, Alabama, in the summer of 1994. That's the same summer that Michael Jordan—yup, His Airness, the basketball player, leading the Chicago Bulls to a jaw-dropping threepeat in 1991-93—retired from basketball and made his debut with the Birmingham Barons. Yup, the B'ham Barons play *base*ball.

Don't get me wrong—Jordan's baseball athleticism was about a jillion times better than anything 99 percent of humans have ever done with a ball and a bat. But it just wasn't his sport. There was no art, no magic, no soaring through the air with impossible hangtime in a baller ballet of his own choreography. We sat sweating in the stands and watched him out there, in right field, I think? Where he seemed . . . not quite at home, a little uneasy, out of sync. (I'm willing to consider that I might have been projecting.)

Anyway, MJ didn't last very long with the Barons, or with baseball generally. He unretired from basketball about as soon as he could and dazzled us with *another* Bulls basketball threepeat, 1996-98. It's like he was *born* to play that game.

That's how Christianity feels to me. I'm not saying I'm the Michael Jordan of Christianity—Christianity is way harder than basketball, and I'm not nearly as gifted as MJ. I mean, like, this is where I'm supposed to be. I know how to *play* it, and I don't mean any disrespect by the use of that word. Rather, like Jordan on the court, Christianity requires all my energy, mental and physical and spiritual; and it makes the best use of every single thing I give to it; and it returns to me buckets of joy and strength and health in the doing of it. I am in sync here. I get incredible hangtime. I was born to play this game, to live this life, to rejoice in this faith, to love this Messiah and everything he loves.

Which is why I want to tell you about Jesus in a hamster ball. And eventually we'll get to Jesus, the Humanest Human. But first, I want to tell you about Jesus, the embodied Logic of God.

Jesus, the Embodied Logic of God

One strange thing about the story of the Bible is that it has *two* "once upon a times." And I don't just mean that Genesis 1 and Genesis 2 offer differing accounts of the coming-into-being-of-all-things that make belief in a literal six-day creation quite impossible. *

The second "once upon a time" I'm talking about is the one that comes very near the end, in terms of when it was penned compared to the rest of the biblical writings: the one in the Gospel of John. John opens with a familiar formula: "In the beginning . . ." Just like Genesis 1:1, right? Which makes John's Gospel an effective rewind

---

* I absolutely appreciate the broader truths communicated by the layering of both creation accounts: that everything that is, is God's idea and called into being by God's own desire; that God finds everything that is adorable; that God imbues human creatures with a bit of God's own Spirit and enlists them as partners, with God and with each other, for the care of each other and this whole adorable world. I'm saying that, taken together, Genesis 1 and Genesis 2 are more *true* than *factual*, if you catch my drift.

into the distant, poetic past, long before there's a pregnant teenager, a barn birth, a wilderness prophet, a messianic ministry. To appreciate all that happens in Jesus's life, John says, we have to get in the Wayback Machine (or the Magic Tree House, you can choose) and set it for "in the beginning." And what—or whom—do we find when we get there? Check it:

> In the beginning was the Word, and the Word was with God, and the Word was God. . . . And the Word became flesh and lived among us, and we have seen his glory, the glory as of a father's only son, full of grace and truth. (John 1:1, 14)

That's right, it's Jesus, the embodied Word of God. If anyone ever asks you, "Do you believe that the Bible is the Word of God?" you can say, "The Bible is my sacred text and contains the testimony of my ancestors in faith concerning their own learnings about the nature and character of God, but 'Word of God' is not really a claim the Bible makes about itself. Indeed, the Bible doesn't even really know itself as we know it, as it didn't exist in canonized form until long after its words had been recorded. But the Bible does say that Jesus is the Word of God. So do you believe that?"

And when they ask you how a person can be a word, you tell them it's all about the Greek philosophy.* Because the word for "Word" in John 1 is, in the Greek of its composition, *logos*. And *logos* is a technical term in philosophy, first developed by my old pal Heraclitus in the late sixth, early fifth centuries BCE. ("Pals" might be overstating, but I think we're friends on Facebook.) *Logos*, the way Heraclitus used it, means something like "ordering principle," like

---

* You can also refer them to Cormac McCarthy's *The Road* (2006), an elegiac, postapocalyptic novel that begins with a father awakening in the dark morning and feeling "each precious breath" of his young, sleeping son. The father murmurs a prayer, or a challenge, into the dawning day: "If he is not the word of God God never spoke."

the way the pieces of the world fit together. An example of a simple *logos*-as-ordering-principle could be the categorization of stuff as animal, vegetable, or mineral.

Aristotle (fourth century BCE, getting closer!) picked up *logos* to use alongside *ethos* and *pathos* as the three interrelated components of effective rhetoric. (If you ever took Public Speaking 101, you already know this.) *Ethos* meant the speaker had to be trustworthy, or at least credible; *pathos* named the reality that humans are moved by appeals to their emotions. The inclusion of *logos* meant, no matter how believable the speaker, no matter how skilled their tugging at the audience's heartstrings, the *ideas* being presented had to *make sense*. Like Heraclitus's "ordering principle," the pieces of one's argument had to fit together. We would say, in our English, the argument should follow *logic*—a word we get from the Greek *logos*. Ta-da!

Now fast-forward to John the Gospeler (last decade of the first century CE), who wants to take his readers back to "once upon a time." He wants to connect what's *about* to happen concerning Jesus of Nazareth with all that has happened *already*, all the way back before time even existed. So: "In the beginning was the *logos*," John says. "In the beginning was the *logic*, the *ordering principle*, the *making sense*."

To dig deep into all that this could mean, consider how many contemporary fields of expertise have a *logos* of their own, manifest as language (words!) that people outside the field don't much understand. For example:

> Architects dream about buildings, then draw their dreams into blueprints. Blueprints are not the building itself, but they are the *logos* of the building, the logic by which the building can come into reality, if someone who knows the *logos* of blueprints sets their hands to it.

> Composers write their dreams into musical scores. The scores

are not the music itself, but they are the *logos* of the music, the logic by which the song can be heard, if someone who knows the *logos* of the notation on the page brings it to life on their instrument. I know musicians who, when reading a score, hear the music in their head, so well do they know the *logos* of that language.

> Football coaches draw plays on a chalkboard for the athletes, *x*'s and *o*'s with enthusiastic arrows showing intentional, coordinated movement by the players. The chalkboard is not the game; it's the *logos* of what the coach imagines could happen, if the athletes embody the logic as they play.

> Medical professionals imagine healing or palliative treatments for diseased or broken bodies, and they write their observations into medical charts. The charts are neither the disease nor the healing, and they are certainly not the human body under discussion (beware of any doctor who spends more time looking at your chart than at *you*). But anyone who understands the *logos* of the numbers and abbreviations in the folder knows quite a lot about the body it describes, and perhaps also what to do next for that body's good.

There are so many more—engineers' schematics for bridges and highways, legislators writing and attorneys applying codified law, my mom making my dad a three-piece suit from whole cloth according to a Butterick pattern, me assembling flatpacks from IKEA into actual furniture with nothing but an Allen wrench and those booklets of instructional graphics. All these symbols and signs meant to communicate ideas, all these words (words!), are cryptic to anyone who doesn't know the *logos*. But to those who do, they are the *logic* by which ideas could come into being—by which dreams could become reality, by which something that exists only in someone's mind could become a thing in the world that everyone else can see.

Now hear John's Gospel say,

In the beginning was the Word [*Logos*, Logic], and the Word [*Logos*, Logic] was with God, and the Word [*Logos*, Logic] was God. . . . And the Word [*Logos*, Logic] became flesh and lived among us, and we have seen his glory, the glory as of a father's only son, full of grace and truth. (John 1:1, 14)

By choosing this word *logos*, John is tapping into this old philosophical idea to say that (a) God has a mind, from which come ideas (everything God wants!); and (b) God's ideas (everything God wants!) get translated into reality by means of God's *logos* or logic or blueprint or playbook or musical score; and (c) God's own logic/blueprint/playbook/score eventually puts on a body ("became flesh") and enters its own creation ("lived among us"); meaning that Jesus is the embodiment of God's logic.

Meaning: You want to know how God thinks, what God imagines, what God dreams about, what God wants? Look at Jesus, who is the walking, talking embodiment of God's own mind. Jesus, God's blueprint for building the world. Jesus, God's score for the music of the cosmos. Jesus, God's Butterick pattern for a very fine three-piece suit made and worn with such love.

Jesus IS everything God wants. Jesus IS *God getting everything God wants.*

I know, right?!!

He is the image of the invisible God, the firstborn of all creation; for in him all things in heaven and on earth were created, things visible and invisible, whether thrones or dominions or rulers or powers—all things have been created through him and for him. He himself is before all things, and in him all things hold together. . . . For *in him all the fullness of God was pleased to dwell.* (Col. 1:15–17, 19, emphasis added, *emphatically!*)

4

JESUS IN A HAMSTER BALL

Just for kicks, I ask you: What did Jesus mostly talk about? In the Gospels, I mean, according to Matthew, Mark, Luke, and John. What was his go-to topic, his biggest deal, the thing he couldn't seem to let go of, tenaciously chewing on it like a dog with a bone?

People offer all kinds of answers. "Salvation" is a biggie, which I suspect is kind of a catch-all word for the way we think Christianity functions for us—how it's *useful*. "Salvation" in this imagining is an antidote for the reality that, left on our own, we humans are kind of a wreck. It's an admission that we need divine help to escape the eternal consequences of the temporary messes we've made. On some level, I don't disagree. Humans are kind of a wreck. Some of the temporary messes we've made have very long-lasting consequences. We are indeed in need of divine help.

I just don't believe anymore that God has prepared an eternal torture chamber for people who get God wrong,* and that being Christian is our best bet for getting God right (eww, no) and escaping God's wrath. At least in my context, that's what people assume salvation is mostly about: being saved from God's own self, God's judgment, God's punishment. They have absorbed the idea that

---

* You could read more about that in Rob Bell's *Love Wins: A Book About Heaven, Hell, and the Fate of Every Person Who Ever Lived* (2011) or David Bentley Hart's *That All Shall Be Saved: Heaven, Hell, and Universal Salvation* (2019).

Christian faith (or more or less regular attendance at Christian-y things) is, above all, "fire insurance" or a "get out of hell free" card, to put it crassly. Some of the most dearly beloveds from my fund-agelical upbringing would say they are Christian so they "can go to heaven." Which is a nicer way of saying the same thing.

But I digress. Because, as it turns out, salvation isn't a topic that comes up much with Jesus, unless he's decrying certain religionists' obsession with it. Like this:

> He called the crowd with his disciples, and said to them, "If any want to become my followers, let them deny themselves and take up their cross and follow me. For those who want to save their life will lose it, and those who lose their life for my sake, and for the sake of the gospel, will save it." (Mark 8:34–35)

It's not a great advertisement for "salvation" if that's what he intends for us to chase after, is it? He literally says the quest for salvation is a losing proposition.

Sometimes, in answer to that question way back there, "What did Jesus mostly talk about?," people say "Sin," imagining Jesus as a roving investigative reporter, a finger-pointing accuser. While it's true that he wasn't afraid to call the balls and strikes of human moral agency, his run-ins with people only sometimes touched on their ethical shortcomings, and then mostly because he was ready to forgive, quick with a gracious erasure of whatever they were most ashamed of, usually without even knowing what it was they'd done or left undone.

He did, however, frequently cast a sharply critical eye on the ugliness of the strict religionists, the hypocrisy embedded in a distorted system that labeled certain people "sinners" while ignoring the corruption in the religionists' own claims to righteousness. See, for example, Matthew 23. Or Mark 7:1–23. Or Luke 13:10–17. *Et cetera.*

Sometimes people say Jesus talked mostly about blessings. Or discipleship. Or suffering. Some folx in my church give the cheeky answer "Where he was gonna eat his next meal," recognizing that Jesus seemed always to be hungry, always seeking out a friendly table for dinner, drink, and dialogue. In light of Isaiah's eschatological vision of the heavenly banquet with rich food and fine wine, I think that's a dandy answer. But not quite right for this exercise; stay with me here.

Jesus Was Obsessed

I don't mean to leave you in suspense by rehearsing the answers I think are not quite right. It's just that I remember my own delight when, after years and years of churchgoing and sermon listening and Bible reading, I learned what Jesus *actually* talks about in the Gospels more than anything else: he just cannot say enough about *the reign, or kingdom, of God.*

There are kajillions of instances of the word "kingdom" in the Gospels, weighted heavily toward Matthew, Mark, and Luke. Matthew uses "kingdom of heaven" because, good Jewish boy that he is, he won't say or write the name of God without a really, really good reason. Mark and Luke (Gentiles without the same scruples) freely use "kingdom of God."

Even John's Gospel, the weird, late little brother of the other Gospels, introduces Jesus in an early story as one who uses "kingdom of God" as a kind of shorthand for what he's mainly about:

Now there was a Pharisee named Nicodemus, a leader of the Jews. He came to Jesus by night and said to him, "Rabbi, we know that you are a teacher who has come from God; for no one can do these signs that you do apart from the presence of God." Jesus answered him, "Very truly, I tell you, no one can see the kingdom of God without being born from above." Nicodemus said to him, "How can anyone be born after having grown old? Can one enter a second time into the mother's womb and be born?" Jesus answered, "Very truly, I tell you, no one can *enter the kingdom of God* without being born of water and Spirit." (John 3:1-5, emphasis mine)

When I talk about Jesus talking this way, I say "reign of God" to unhook God from a gendered term; God can be a king or a queen or both or neither, so "reign" works nicely. And it helps us English speakers too, because for us a kingdom is a geopolitical entity, a bounded geography with monarchic governance—either that, or a fictional, Disney-esque fairy-tale setting with princesses and magic spells and ridiculous ballgowns for everyday wear.

But for Jesus, "kingdom" was conceptual rather than geographic. It's the state of being that accompanies the king/queen/sovereign. And what does the king/queen/sovereign get? Whatever the king/queen/sovereign wants! And if God is that king/queen/sovereign, if God is in charge, then *God gets whatever God wants*. And, to Jesus's way of thinking, this was the only news worth sharing.

So Jesus had all these quirky ways to help us know what the reign of God *is*, by telling us what it's *like*. "It's like a little seed!" he would say excitedly. "You dig a tiny hole in the dirt, you drop it in, you cover it up and give it some water, and then you go to bed! And when you get up in the morning, it has grown, you know not how! [Mark 4:26-27] Reign of God, everybody!" He looks around, eyebrows raised expectantly, waiting for the oohs and aahs. His hearers scratch their heads, furrow their brows.

He tries again: "It's like my mom making bread! She measures the flour by the fistful, and shakes in a little yeast! It only takes a little, and the whole dough is leavened! [Matt. 13:33] Just like the reign of God! Ta-da!" But his students look confused, and a little worried.

He tries again and again: "It's like a gorgeous pearl, more beautiful than anything you've seen up to now, so you pawn everything you own—your lawnmower, your kids' bikes, whatever you can find—so you can buy it! [Matt. 13:45-46]

"Or like a treasure so rich you dig a deep hole in someone else's field and bury it, then pawn all your stuff and buy that field come morning! [Matt. 13:44]

"Or like a coin a woman lost, and she stayed up all night sweeping till she found it and got it back in her purse, then threw a late-night house party for all her friends to celebrate! [Luke 15:8-9]

"Or like a dad whose rotten son comes home, finally, and the dad rushes down the driveway to meet him! It'll make the other son mad, but the dad isn't worried, see?! [Luke 15:11-32]

"It's like a shrub! [Mark 4:30-32]

"It's like a farmer! [Mark 4:3]

"It's like a vineyard! [Matt. 20:1-16]

"It's like an investor! [Matt. 25:14-30]

"It's like a farm worker! [Matt. 13:24-30]

"It's like a banquet! [Luke 14:16-24]

"It's like a wedding! [Matt. 22:1-14]

"It's like a bridesmaid! [Matt. 25:1-13]

"It's like a fishing net!" [Matt. 13:47-50]

In my imagination Jesus is very enthusiastic (!!!) as he spins out these images, because they make perfect sense to him, and more than anything he wants his friends to get on board with his obsession. He wants to help them see what he sees: that despite all appearances to the contrary, *God is in charge. God gets everything God wants! (!!!)*

Mark, likely the first guy to take a stab at writing a thing called a "gospel" (not really a biography, not really a history, but a special subgenre that was its own thing, sufficient to communicate the identity of Jesus by testifying to what he said, did, and suffered), said that Jesus returned to civilization after his forty days in the desert with nothing but the reign of God on his mind.

Now after John was arrested, Jesus came to Galilee, proclaiming the good news of God, and saying, "The time is fulfilled, and the kingdom of God has come near; repent, and believe in the good news." (Mark 1:14–15)

Or, with a little tweaking on my part:

Now after John was arrested, Jesus came home, preaching the gospel of God, saying, "Here we go! The reign of God is right here, so close you can reach out and touch it!* It will change your life, and trust me when I say that this is *good* news!"

So the reign of God = the *gospel* of God, and "gospel" means "good news." God being in charge, God's sovereignty, God getting everything God wants, is meant to be *good news*—the best you've ever heard. So good you'd sell everything you have, throw a party, call your friends, change your life, reconfigure everything you've ever wanted, just to have a piece of it.

But still: what is it, again? With the original disciples, we squinch our eyes and tilt our heads, trying to see what Jesus sees. Seeds, shrubs, sowers. Pearls, parties, prodigals come home. "But what is any of that to me?" you could ask, as I have asked. "How is it *news*, again? Because I'm kind of a wreck, Jesus. I've done some shit. Some shit has been done to me. I need saving, you know? Not like a 'get out of hell free' card I can carry around till Death has its way with me, but right here, right now. Got anything for that?"

Jesus sighs. The metaphors aren't working as well as he'd hoped.** "OK," he says, regrouping for a new strategy. "We're not

---

* "So close you can reach out and touch it," because the Greek metaphor is "at hand." The New Revised Standard Version says, "The kingdom of God has come *near*," but "near" drains the poetry, dang it.

** Or maybe it's a sigh of satisfaction because they're working exactly as he expected, exactly as he needed them to, hammering home the reality that the communicating all that well here. Why don't I stop talking, and just show you?" And he takes off at a brisk clip, trusting that you're right behind him. No time for goodbyes or long-term planning; just drop your stuff and hustle up.

That's when you first realize that Jesus travels in a messiah-sized hamster ball.

The Image You Didn't Know You Needed

You gotta picture Jesus, walking, walking, walking, endless days of walking through Galilee and Samaria and Judea; and for our purposes here, you gotta picture him walking in a hamster ball. Not a hamster *wheel*—those sad, squeaky treadmills that keep caged hamsters running fruitlessly toward the happily they are ever after*—but a hamster *ball*—the clear plastic sphere that unscrews into halves, into which your hamster scampers gladly, halves then locked together to enclose the hamster, so the hamster can roll around your house without getting wedged behind the fridge or slobbered on by the dog or squashed by people-feet. (There are air holes so the hamster, or in our case, Jesus, can breathe freely.)

What I'm trying to say is, Jesus doesn't only *talk* about the reign of God; Jesus travels in an atmospheric bubble of the reign of God. He is surrounded by God-getting-everything-God-wants-ness. God's reign is all around him, behind and before him. He breathes it. He *exudes* it. When it comes to God getting everything God wants, *that's how Jesus rolls.*

Which means that wherever Jesus is, God is getting everything

---

reign of God, like everything about God, is not quite *graspable* by us. We don't have words for it all because if we did, if we could wrap our tiny minds around it, it wouldn't be *God*. It's no good to try and explain God or God's reign straight on; these are truths you have to tell *slant*. See Matthew 13:13. See also Emily Dickinson, "Tell all the truth but tell it slant."

* Lyle Lovett, "Her First Mistake" (1996): "I just keep on running faster / Chasing the happily I am ever after." Describes a lot of life, doesn't it?

God wants. "The reign of God is so close you can reach out and touch it," he said back in Mark 1:14-15, remember? "It's *right here*." And he gestures around himself, at the hamster ball of God's reign he travels in.

The hamster ball visual is helpful for capturing the 3D-ness of it, but it quickly fails because the plastic is not permeable. What we need to lay hold of in our mind's eye is Jesus traveling in a reign-of-God *cloud*. Like the hamster ball, it goes everywhere he goes; but the edges are less defined, more traversable. More like a *billow*, an atmospheric anomaly that goes where he goes, like that kid in the Charlie Brown comics who was always in need of a bath.

So let's go with Jesus enveloped in a fog of Axe Body Spray. Like, he's wearing a strong scent-cloud so potent that you can smell him coming and still smell him after he's passed on by.* Jesus's favored Axe scent is Limited Edition: Reign of God. He doesn't have to spray it on; he just wakes up that way.

The permeability of the reign-of-God Axe cloud means, if you get close enough to Jesus, you enter the reign-of-God region, a portable zone where God is getting everything God wants, and whatever God wants happens to *you*. Step into Jesus's bubble, and—

—If your body or mind is broken or sick, in the reign-of-God cloud around Jesus you get restored to health and made strong (Mark 5:25-29, for example).

—If you are hungry, for food or justice, you get fed with whatever you are hungriest for (John 6:1-14, for example).

—If you are lonely and isolated from community, you get relationship, a return to family and friends and synagogue (Luke 17:11-14, for example, and really all the healings of physical maladies that kept the sick person segregated from the community).**

---

* Absolutely no offense intended to people who wear this actual product. You have your reasons.

** I think the sweetest story about Jesus solving loneliness is in Luke 7:11-15, where Jesus raises the Nain widow's only son from death, and when the kid

—If you are weighed down by guilt or shame, you get mercy and dignity, the restoration of your unashamed self, a clean slate (John 8:1-11, for example).

—If something wicked has ahold of you, something you can't get free of on your own, you get liberation (Mark 3:9-11, for example).

—If you don't know which way to go, if you're stuck with no inkling of how to move on from here, you get clarity and guidance and a brand-new sense of direction for a fresh start (Matt. 4:19; 8:22; 9:9, for example).

All you have to do is get close to him, inside the reign-of-God sphere he carries with him. Touch him, or even just his clothing. Or let him touch you, or speak to you, or rub spit in your eyes, or pinch your tongue, or put his fingers in your ears, or even just *think* about you for a second, and whatever God wants is going to become reality for you. That's the gospel. That's the good news of God's reign—*God gets everything God wants*—that Jesus is so obsessed with.

*Preach the Gospel; If Necessary, Use Words**

Remember a few pages back, where Mark's Gospel showed us Jesus coming out of the desert after forty days with nothing but the reign of God on his mind? Here it is again, just in case:

> Now after John was arrested, Jesus came to Galilee, proclaiming the good news of God, and saying, "The time is fulfilled, and the kingdom of God has come near; repent, and believe in the good news." (Mark 1:14-15)

---

comes to life, Luke says, "Jesus gave him to his mother." I'm a mom; I can imagine how that felt. The defeat of Death—even, ultimately, our own resurrection—is about the restoration of relationship.

* Saint Francis of Assisi may or may not have said this. I don't know, and the internets don't agree. Still, it's interesting, and gives rise to thought.

Those verses are the Gospel of Mark's "programmatic state-ment." Every Gospel has one, and they're all different. The pro-grammatic statements clue the reader in to what the gospeler will be drawing our attention to in the rest of their account. Careful readers pay close attention to the programmatic statement in each Gospel to appreciate each one's unique take on all that Jesus says, does, and suffers.*

From Mark's programmatic statement, then, we would expect Je-sus to be a *preacher* above all else. "Proclaiming" in the translation I'm using** is actually "preaching," so we're looking for the Jesus of Mark's account to be articulate, wordy, and just narcissistic enough to think that people will listen to him. (Maybe I'm projecting. Again.)

But when you read Mark's Gospel, you notice that Jesus ac-tually doesn't talk all that much, compared to Matthew, Luke, and John. There's no Sermon on the Mount (Matthew) or on the Plain (Luke) in Mark; no long discourses on his own iden-tity (John). If you had one of those Bibles with all Jesus's words printed in red, you could see it easily. Mark's Jesus is pretty tight-lipped for someone whose programmatic statement introduces him as a preacher.

What if, though, Mark means for the reader to reconsider what "preaching" actually consists of? What if it's on purpose that his programmatic statement identifies Jesus as a preacher, then barely has him string two sentences together for the rest of the book? What if we are meant to understand that the *preaching* of the reign of God is happening every time someone steps into the rolling cloud of God-getting-everything-God-wants that Jesus carries with him? It's not (only) what he *says*; it's (also) what he *does*. Jesus preaches the reign of God by doing (manifesting, embodying, bringing to

---

* In Matthew, it's mostly agreed that 5:17–20 is the programmatic statement. In Luke, it's 4:16–21. In John . . . well, like a lot of things with John, it's hard to say. I would argue for John 1:14.

** The New Revised Standard Version, natch.

life) the reign of God everywhere he goes.* He is not only the Logos/ Logic of God; he is the *embodied* Logic of God. Everywhere he goes, God gets everything God wants. Thanks be to God!

Unless . . .

* I am entirely indebted to Brian K. Blount's *Go Preach!: Mark's Kingdom Message and the Black Church Today* (1998) for this insight. Dr. Blount invigorated my reading of Mark and my practice of the Christian faith with this book.

5

JUST ONE JESUS, JUST ONE FUTURE

We should pause here. Let's take a step back from all the celebrating, all the hallelujahs and "sweet Jesuses!" that ring out wherever he's just been, and recognize that not everyone is so happy with his reign-of-God-scented cloud. It turns out, there are some things you can bring into proximity of Jesus that you might have wanted to keep just the same, because the status quo is absolutely working for you. "Nah, Jesus, I'm good," you might try to demur, backing up as his hamster ball rolls closer. But the embodied Logic of God has something to say about that status quo. Get too close to Jesus, and—

— If you are *powerful,* he wrestles you to the ground without lifting a finger (Matt. 15:1-14, for example).

— If you are *privileged,* he cuts you down to size (Luke 18:18-25, for example).

— If you are *prejudiced,* he surrounds you with people you don't like (Luke 7:36-50, for example).

— If you are *proud,* he exposes your flaws (Luke 10:25-37, for example).

I don't know why they all start with *p*. They just do.

Here's the important thing to notice, and I cannot italicize this hard enough: *it's the same Axe cloud, the same hamster ball, the same reign-of-God aura around Jesus* that makes some people jump with joy and has some other people throwing up a little in their mouth

53

and plotting to eliminate him from the face of the earth. How you feel when you get near him depends on what you bring to the situation, you know? Because whatever you bring into proximity of *God getting everything God wants*, it's going to be transformed. And fair warning: that transformation might hurt. It might take some egg breaking to get that reign-of-God omelet, right? Transformation requires some demolition.

Which is why, perhaps, Jesus said back in Mark 1:15, "*Change your life* (repent) so that this will be *good* news for you" (another possible rendering of that verse). It's news either way, that God is in charge despite all appearances to the contrary and is getting everything God wants. But it's *good* news, or not, depending on what you bring into proximity of it.

Good News? Depends.

Here's my favorite example of that proximity-to-Jesus thing at work in a Gospel story. In Mark 2:1–12—just the very next minute after he's started preaching (saying and doing) the reign of God—he's in a little house in Capernaum, "speaking the word (the *logos*!) to them." Mark doesn't bother to tell us what Jesus is saying; Mark is in too much of a hurry to show us what Jesus is doing.

It's super crowded up in that house. There's a man who can't walk and (maybe?) wishes he could, but he couldn't get through the wall of people even if he were ambulatory. So his friends hoist him up on top of the house, and with their knives and their hands they chop through the roof till clods and thatch are raining down on Jesus's head. When a big enough chunk of it gives way, they lower their guy through the hole to Jesus's feet.* Somehow they know:

---

* It would be worth noticing here that Jesus says nary a word about the property damage the house incurs. Not a whisper that "someone will have to pay for that roof" and "someone will have to repair that house" and "someone will have to clean up this mess," and "why don't those thugs have any respect for what they just have to get him close to Jesus, inside that hamster ball of God's reign, and something good will happen.

Jesus rewards their effort on so many levels. There are so many beautiful things happening, I'm going to make a list. You should definitely read the story so you'll know if my list is trustworthy.

1. Jesus takes note of the little community of people who have conspired to get the guy to him. Mark says, "When he saw *their* faith"—that is, the ones looking down at him through the hole in the roof. In Jesus's reign-of-God bubble, community is noted and honored and powerful.

2. Jesus calls the man in front of him "Son." It's a lovely habit he has of calling people by relational names—"son," "daughter," "child," even sometimes "friend." In Jesus's reign-of-God atmosphere, everybody is related to someone, even the loneliest hearts.

3. Jesus serves up a heaping helping of mercy. "Son, your sins are forgiven," he says. That's likely not what anybody thought he would offer to a guy whose mobility impairment was the presenting issue. But we're invited to trust that in the reign-of-God cloud around Jesus, what's most broken is what's getting repaired. It's not the man's mobility impairment that Jesus sees as primary.

4. The VRPs, the Very Religious Persons, in this case "the scribes"—guys whose job it was to copy scripture word for word, and who therefore were deferred to as experts in the little-*w* words of God—ironically cannot recognize the capital-W Word of God standing right in front of them. They grouse that this Jesus has transgressed religious boundaries, treading into territory that

---

decent, hard-working people have built?" Nope, not a word. For Jesus, it's people and their pain over property and its protection. Just sayin', here in the spring, summer, and fall of 2020 with protests in full swing against racist policing and racist policy and the racist ordering of all things US American.

is reserved for God alone: that is, the work of absolving sinners, the work of mercy.

Uh-oh—in our list, one of those things is not like the others. It's a real feel-good miracle right up to the moment somebody decides to defend the status quo, the way things have always been, the way we've always done it. And the thing I really want you to grab hold of here is that Jesus has only done *one* thing—one miracle of mercy, the liberation of one man from his shame—and that *one* thing is the best thing that ever happened to one guy, but to some other guys it's triggering a spiritual migraine.

Same Jesus. Same cloud. Same reign of God.

Jesus, who has this weird Spidey-sense when people are complaining about him, addresses the VRPs with a sticky rhetorical question I've never heard satisfactorily answered. "Which is harder?" he asks. Or, "Which is less likely, least possible, in your VRP opinion? Mercy or miraculous healing?" Could go either way.

Jesus then shows that in his rarefied atmosphere, both are possible; not even difficult, really; he hasn't broken a sweat. "Get on up, go on home," he tells the guy. The man stands up, clicks his heels together three times, and goes home, presumably to people who love him and will be happy to have him back. Everybody watches him go, jaws hanging open, and we note their amazement, because everything that has just happened has blown their tiny minds, and ours. Everybody's gonna be talking about what happened here for a long, long time.

It's the same Jesus, same cloud, same atmosphere of God's reign. It's the Best Day Ever for the guy on the mat, but it goes over like a lead balloon with the (proud, prejudiced, privileged, powerful) VRPs.

"God gets everything God wants," Jesus says. "It's happening now, if you get close enough to me. News, yes. Good? Depends."

Heaven? or Hell?

The most deeply embedded piece of unhelpful Christian doctrine that sneaks its way into Galileo Church, the one that most fully obscures the absolute fabulousness of God Getting Everything God Wants as hoped for by the prophets and demonstrated by Jesus, is the one about heaven and hell.

Somehow in the twenty-first century lots of us still loosely imagine a three-tiered universe with heaven "up there" and hell "down there." This doctrine requires Christians to believe that God stands ready to reward God's favorites with eternal residence in a tricked-out vacation resort where choral singing is universally loved, and equally ready (even *more* ready!) to punish everybody else with eternal torture in a flaming, sulfurous dungeon. Yeah, that's right: hell smells like farts.

In some versions of the Christian heaven-'n'-hell geography, the souls ensconced in each place can *see* each other. It makes hell that much more hellish, to witness the everlasting party upstairs. And doesn't it say a lot about us if we imagine that *knowing* about the inescapable suffering of our human siblings makes us enjoy heaven all the more? It's (mostly) not true about me now, that I get off on other people's pain. Will it be true about me in the future of God's imagining, assuming (fingers crossed!) that I'm in God's good stead at the moment I breathe my last and get my ticket punched for The Good Place? *Should* it?

Come on, y'all.

What if we could admit that none of our ancestors in faith really had any idea what happens to people when they die? What if the ones who spoke of the eternal destiny of humans in the afterlife (understanding that not every biblical ancestor even *believed* in an afterlife) were speaking about it, as in so many cases of Things Too Hard for Human Brains to Grasp, in metaphors? "Pearly gates," "fiery lake," "streets of gold," "many mansions," "weeping and gnashing of teeth". . . What if they meant to say something like, "There's more to life than *this* life, because God won't abandon us to the brokenness and burdens of this life. And human decisions in this life have consequences for whatever 'more' there is. There is a way to live this life that is in harmony with God's desires for the universe, and a way to live this life that is discordant with God's future; and it matters which you choose."

Because here is something I think the Bible shows us from cover to cover, as represented in that story of the man-formerly-known-as-paralyzed in Mark 2:1-12. The thing is, when the reign of God happens near you, when God getting everything God wants happens *to* you, that's either The Best Day Ever or it smells like farts. Same Jesus, same mercy, same moment—different people, different dispositions, different reactions.

That is to say, if the arc of the moral universe bends toward justice (i.e., love in public), if this whole shebang is headed toward the future of God's dreams, and *it's just one future* for everything and everyone in the world, one happily-ever-after ending, what if the heaven-or-hell-ness of it is *actually about you* and what kind of person you have become over the course of your lifetime?

Like, if you have learned to love it when God gets something God wants, a bit of justice for the oppressed here, a bit of kindness for the unloved there, a whole heap of mercy slathered over all our brokenness, massive burdens lifted off the backs of the heavy laden; if you've invested your energies in getting/making/doing more of that kind of stuff; then *when* God gets everything God wants, that'll be heaven for you!

And if instead you've spent your life thinking a lot about what you want, and to hell with everybody else; if you've invested a lot of energy in preserving a status quo that works quite nicely for you (pride? privilege? power? prejudice?); well, shoot. In that case, it may well be that when God gets everything God wants, that's gonna hurt like hell.

It's kinda like that little joke Jesus told about wealthy people like us* in Mark 10:25-27. He said, and I'm paraphrasing here, "Oh sure, rich people *can* get into the kingdom of God, because God gets everything God wants! God can even thread a whole camel through the eye of a sewing needle (and without reading glasses!). But have you *seen* that camel after God does what it takes to cram it through that little hole?" Sure, rich people get "in" to God's future, Jesus says. But they don't look so good once they're there. Ouch.

This is the way I'm able to make sense of all the different things the Bible says about the eternal destiny of human beings: we, along with the whole creation, are in motion toward the fullness of God's reign, and decisions we're making now, the ways we are cooperating or not with God's renovation of the cosmos, make all the difference in how it'll seem to us when God gets everything God wants. Heaven, or hell—we're deciding every day.

But What about Grandma?

It's at this point, usually, that a Galileo person who's hearing this idea for the first time will say, "OK, but what about my grandma? Where is she now?" Which I totally get. Both of my beloved grandmothers died within the last several years, and I want very much to imagine them "in heaven," with God, whatever that looks like.

If we were to let go of the idea that "heaven" and "hell" are separate places in a cosmic geography—not only the "upness" and "down-

---

* You may not think of yourself as wealthy, and maybe you're not—I don't know you. But if you bought this book, and drove your car through a drive-through to get a coffee or a Diet Coke to drink while you read it, and settled down with book and drink in your home with multiple rooms and indoor plumbing, maybe you could consider that you are *way* richer than most of the people who have ever lived, ever in the history of the whole wide world? I'm not picking on you. It's just our habit at Galileo Church to not let each other pretend we're not wealthy, we first-worlders. Even when we're broke. Broke is not the same as poor.

ness" of them but also, more generally, the "placeness" of them—would it be possible for us to grok that *time*, too, is a metaphor in this conversation? I say "ultimately" or "finally" or "someday" or "in the future" when God gets everything God wants, as if God exists in linear time like we do, with each moment leading to the next moment, so that existence stretches out in an orderly progression from "Once upon a time" to "happily ever after." But what if that's not actually true for God? What if, for God and for everyone who has departed this space-time continuum (i.e., died), God *already has gotten* everything God wants?

Then your deceased grandma, and both of mine, could be resting contentedly in the very heart of Very God, smack in the middle of the "future" (to us) of God's imagining, their own hearts very happy because their whole lives were dedicated to God getting everything God wants.

It's at this point, then, that someone might be brave enough to admit that their grandma wasn't exactly, uh, heart-of-God-ready. She was a little bit racist, maybe. Frugal to the point of stingy. A busybody. Bitter, abusive, protectionistic, and a conspiracy theory aficionado. "But we loved her, still. She was always sweet to us kids, and I could tell her anything." So . . . lake of fire for dearly departed Granny?

Welp. God have mercy on the grandmas, and everybody else, who are bundles of contradictions. So broken, so burdened, and yet so beloved. I have presided at funerals for the meanest people, whose well-known addictions and adulteries and avarice were stacked in layers over the decades, only to watch family and friends genuinely mourn their passing, as if the deceased did *not* make other people's lives a hell for much of the time they were alive. I don't think it's sentimentalism, and I don't think it's (all) attributable to people's metagrief over capital-*D* Death. I think we humans have the capacity to love people whose rottenness and loveliness coexist like a soft-serve swirl of chocolate and vanilla. Maybe because most of us are self-aware enough to know we're swirly like that too.

Maybe also because we've experienced that a lot of our broken-ness comes from the heavy burdens we've had to carry. We sin, to some extent, because we've been sinned against. Not 100 percent the case, but it's worth considering, especially since Jesus said we could remind God that we've been wronged too whenever we make our confessions. "Forgive us our sins as we forgive those who've sinned against us," we pray in language he gave us. Like we're reminding God to remember how hard it is down here.

And if we can love people in all their complexity, graciously un-derstanding that most people are mostly doing the best they can, even people who mostly suck, then why would we imagine God cannot? God knows who our grandmas were, all that they suffered, all that they loved. God has mercy aplenty for them, as for us. The biblical prophets spoke of God's somewhat brutal "refinement" of persons and systems (e.g., Isa. 48:10; Jer. 9:7; Mal. 3:2). There is some thought that perhaps God's final act of mercy for each of us is to purge us of whatever remains in us that's not fit for God's future. Maybe that's what all that fire is about. *

I Don't Actually Know

I'm not claiming to know more than I know here. But I'm pressing the point that scripture itself allows more than one imagining of what comes after this life, when God gets everything God wants. And it's all imaginative speculation because the only person we know who

---

* See also 1 Peter 1:7, where, in the end, a person's faith can be "tested by fire" like precious metals are purified by melting the dross out of them. See also the TV show *The Good Place* (NBC, four seasons, 2016–2020), where the whole system of heaven-'n'-hell is thrown into question, as it examines what kind of hu-man behavior is provoked by that kind of binary thinking. I'm not saying *The*

spent any time in a life after this one and came back to tell about it
. . . didn't talk about it at all.* I suspect that was because (a) there's
just no way to tell us time-bound, space-bound meatbags what it's
like *beyond* without making our heads explode, and (b) what ultimately happens to us was never the main point anyway. God gets
everything God wants, and that's supposed to be enough to go on.

Is it enough for you? That is the question. And it's a damn good
one.

Good Place should tell us what to believe about God, the universe, and everything; but it definitely exposes the ugliness and absurdity in the traditional
Christian doctrine.

* You know what Jesus wanted to talk about when he came back from the dead to
visit his friends for a few weeks? Check it out, from Acts 1:3: "After his suffering he presented himself alive to them by many convincing proofs, appearing
to them during forty days and speaking about the *kingdom of God*" (emphasis
added). Are you surprised? Please tell me you're not surprised.

PART THREE

WHEN GOD DOESN'T GET EVERYTHING GOD WANTS

6

KEYS TO THE KINGDOM

This morning before I sat down to write (OK, this morning as I did every single thing I could think of to procrastinate sitting down to write), I did a few dishes while I listened to the news on the radio. And, as happens many mornings in the Year of Our Lord 2020, it wasn't long before I was weeping into the dishwater.

It was not the initial report of the fire at the Moria refugee camp on the Greek island of Lesbos that did it. I mean, it is truly awful, what happened there: thirteen thousand mostly Afghan refugees crammed into space made for a quarter as many, most of whom had been there for a year or more. Fires swept through the tent camp as refugees fled on foot, carrying everything they own in sacks, aware that they should be careful, as COVID-19 outbreaks have been widespread in their camp.

But I didn't cry until they played a snippet of tape, a few words from an Afghan man who escaped the fire. He didn't add much to the details of what happened, but his exhausted voice, raspy from smoke, simply said in broken English what I suddenly knew was very true: "Nobody care. Nobody care."[*]

Nobody care. Nobody care.

---

[*] Joanna Kakissis, "Fire At Refugee Camp In Greece Was A Disaster Waiting To Happen," *Morning Edition*, NPR, September 10, 2020, https://www.npr.org /2020/09/10/911349863/fire-at-refugee-camp-in-greece-was-a-disaster-waiting -to-happen.

How can this be true? If God gets everything wants, how can refugee camps burn to ash, making double refugees of those who lived there? "Why don't we live in a refugee camp?" I asked my spouse. He sighed. Then we both stood still and quiet for a minute. No answer we've ever heard in church or read in the Bible satisfies. There is no answer. If you say, "There but for the grace of God go I," I'll smack you. (Metaphorically, of course.) The grace or goodness of God, the *virtue* of God, is completely disproven by the Moria fire.

Isn't it?

Jesus Gives It Away

Every time I remember this again, I gasp:

> But he answered them, "You give them something to eat." (Mark 6:37a)

Or this:

> "I will give you the keys of the kingdom of heaven, and whatever you bind on earth will be bound in heaven, and whatever you loose on earth will be loosed in heaven." (Matt. 16:19)

Or this:

> He breathed on them and said to them, "Receive the Holy Spirit. If you forgive the sins of any, they are forgiven them; if you retain the sins of any, they are retained." (John 20:22b–23)

Or this:

> *The whole freakin' book of Acts.*

Did you know it's pretty unlikely that Jesus's ministry lasted three years, as some of us were taught,* and it's much more likely that his entire magical mystery tour of Galilee and Judea really took more like eight or nine months? In which case, that little band of friends who followed him around had a very short but *very* intense internship with the savior of the world, at the end of which he looked at all of them and said, "Yep, you got this; y'all can pick it up from here." And before they (we!) could say, "Uh, are you sure?" he was gone, baby, gone.

They didn't have a very good track record up to that moment. They had *not*, in fact, "give[n] [anybody] [anything] to eat." Upon being handed the keys to the kingdom they promptly ran it into a ditch, or at least Peter** did, by his insistence that Jesus was not gonna suffer on his watch, by gum. Then when Jesus's suffering began in earnest, his closest friends, including Peter, mostly ditched him. The womenfolk stayed, of course; women are not deterred from love by pain, their own or other people's, for better or for worse.***

But here's the deal, and the part that makes me gasp: when Jesus came back around after all that suffering, he looked up the *very same people*. They weren't hard to find; they were basically too freaked out to leave the room where they had eaten their last meal

---

* Three years is a guess, based on the Gospel of John's report of Jesus celebrating three Passovers during his ministry (John 2:13; 6:4; 13:1). But it's more likely, as in Matthew, Mark, and Luke, that he celebrated only one Passover with his friends at the end of his ministry, when he traveled to Jerusalem for a final confrontation with religious and imperial leaders. John is a special flower; you know that, right? He does what he wants, tells his story his own way. And we love him for it.

** My opinion about Peter is that he is forever the only one brave enough to say what they're all thinking, so he's the one who gets in trouble all the time. I stan Peter.

*** A gross generalization, I know. But isn't it truer than we would like it to be?

with him last Thursday. On finding them, he huffed and puffed and blew the Holy Spirit right into their lives, telling them it was time to get up, get out, and get started on the work he was leaving for them. What he had done for that man on the mat in Mark 2:1–12 was now their job description. *Get out there and start forgiving! healing! putting the broken world back together!*

What made him think they could do any better now than they had before? With respect to the forgiveness thing, it actually didn't work out very well at all, right at first. Remember Ananias and Sapphira in Acts 5, the ones who did a real estate deal and gave only half the profits to the church, pretending they wrote a check for the whole thing? *Kaboom!* And *kaboom* again! Those two were hauled out feetfirst to wherever the early church hid their bodies. I can imagine the called church leadership meeting they had the next day, an emergency debate on whether that's how Jesus meant for them to take care of his business. I'm glad they decided it wasn't. Ananias and Sapphira might have wished they had decided that a little earlier.

It's a thing we know about Jesus, though, if we're paying close attention to the Gospels: he gives away power like he's got it to spare. Though he is infused with and surrounded by the very reign of God, though he can manipulate nature so that sick people become healthy and death works backward and the surface tension of water holds his weight, he is always ready to shuck the credit and congratulate someone else.

"Your faith has made you well," he told countless healees. And I think if I'd been there I'd have probed that one a bit after the crowds had gone home. (Yes, that's right, in the movie in my mind, I am Peter.) "What did you mean when you told them *their* faith was the magic ingredient in their healing? Cuz I was right there, Jesus, and I've seen quite a few of these over the months, and I'm very sure it's nothing special in these sick folx that's, uh, contributory to their own wellness. Come on, you can level with us. It's really just you, right, Lord?"

And in this imagined conversation between the Lord and me, he would say something like this: "Argh! How much longer must I be with you? How much longer must I put up with you?" (Matt. 17:17). What he would mean is, he's been showing us all along that the reign of God is like *this*, like *him*; and how can we not already understand that God gets everything God wants, and one of the things God has always wanted, from the very start, is *partnership* with people?

God doesn't just want people as manipulable playthings, or people as obedient automatons, or people as loyal puppies. God wants real people with real agency to come alongside God and *contribute*. Yes, the cosmos is headed toward a future of God's imagining, and there will come a time (as there have been times before) that God finally has to take the wheel and drive this thing home. But between now and then, God would really appreciate and even enjoy letting someone else drive sometimes too.

So: "Here are the keys to the kingdom," Jesus says, dangling them in front of his disciples like a trusting parent giving the car keys to a teenager with a learner's permit still warm from the DMV laser printer. Which, I'd just like to point out, *he did not have to do*. Nothing prescribed that he had to go and leave it all with them, with us. Once he was raised from the dead, I'm figuring he could do anything he wanted. *Literally. Anything.* But what he wanted was to give it all away. If those ding-dong disciples drove all those months of his hamster-ball-reign-of-God demonstration right into the ground, well, that was a risk he was willing to take.

And maybe we should not have been surprised. I've already somewhere intimated that God's opening gambit with the people God created was to invite them into partnership. "Work with me here!" God invited, giving the first humans spades and rakes and naming rights. "Work with me here!" Jesus invited, giving much later humans those kingdom keys.

What that means about God is that while God has very strong ideas about how the world should work, God is, for now, content to keep inviting humanity into the process of getting it just right. Even though that means God is not always, or even often, getting everything God wants. Not now. Not yet. Because . . .

Nobody care. Nobody care.

Because as much as it hurts God's heart for God's world to suffer, God keeps hoping we will care as much as God does.* And that our care will drive us to work our asses off alongside God, bending the arc of the moral universe degree by degree toward justice (love in public). And if the scriptures testify how very near Jesus's followers came to driving the reign of God right off a cliff, they also testify to the ways in which they sometimes got it exactly, breathtakingly *right*. See the next chapter, "Something, Something, Holy Spirit."

This is our pneumatology** at Galileo Church, which we copied from Jesus, who copied it from God: we are all grown-ass adults here, all of us imbued with the Spirit of the living Christ; which means we have incredible capacity to do incredibly lovely things. We don't, always. But when we do, it is amazing to behold.

---

* Someone has called this quality of God, God's "chronic naivete," as illuminated in the parable of the wicked tenants, Mark 12:1–12, in which the landowner keeps sending messengers who are brutalized and killed by the tenants, and finally reasons, "They will respect my son." Spoiler alert: they do not. But this, Jesus says, is what the reign of God is like. He should know.

** Pneumatology = fancy word for what we think is going on with the Holy Spirit, that mysterious third person of the Trinity.

7

SOMETHING, SOMETHING, HOLY SPIRIT

Behold! Acts 10.

Here is Cornelius, a Gentile, meaning *not* one of God's select favorites, meaning outside any covenant God has ever made with
anybody since Noah—and yet "one of the good ones," they liked to
say about him, because he prayed to their God and gave money
to their poor. And here is an angel of God, telling him he'd better send for somebody named Peter, because the good news of
God's reign is coming closer, getting so close he can reach out and
touch it.

Here is Peter, the aforementioned mouthy disciple, praying
through the noon hour, preoccupied with what someone will make
him for lunch. (He takes after Jesus in this way?) Here is a vision, or
maybe a dream, if there's a difference, in which the sky releases a
giant picnic blanket filled with nonkosher foods, or at least the animals from which such foods could come with the help of a butcher.
Here is hungry-dream Peter resisting the temptation; here is the
voice that accompanies the sheet arguing back, saying, "God gets
everything God wants, don't you get it?" or something close to that.
Here is Peter, awaking to a knock on the door.

Here are Cornelius's messengers with an invitation; here are
Peter's friends; here they all go down together from Joppa to Cae-

sarea. Here is Cornelius's whole household, ready to listen; here is Peter, ready to talk. Here is Peter talking. And talking. And talking.

Here is the Holy Spirit—the very Spirit of the living Christ, tired of Peter talking—interrupting (Acts 10:44) with gifts. Here are *familiar* gifts: Cornelius and his people are Pentecostal, now, which Peter and his friends recognize from just the other day in Jerusalem. Here is Peter asking, "Can anybody think of a good reason not to baptize them?" Here is a new baptismal litany for an entirely new circumstance. And here is Cornelius, dripping wet, now Peter's brother, and Peter his. Here is the world, having never felt so full of promise.

Behold! Acts 11.

Here are the Very Religious Persons, a designation we can now use for the hardcore Jesus people back in Jerusalem, getting wind of the gossip: Peter has eaten with Gentiles. Not that he's baptized them; maybe that's less of a scandal than the fact that, in the spirit of siblinghood, Peter stayed at C's house a while and dipped from a common bowl whatever food they provided. Here they are, saying to Peter, "It's just not *done*. We have to have *standards.*"

Here is Luke, the writer of Acts, having Peter tell the whole entire story all over again, just in case any among his readers missed it the first time. Here is Peter, remembering: Joppa, praying, sheet, voice, triple resistance; Cornelius, Caesarea, vision, invitation, travel; me speaking, Holy Spirit interrupting, Cornelius's kin gifted, me recognizing, resistance overcome, baptisms all around. Here is Peter asking, "What did you want me to do? *Because we all know God gets everything God wants.*" Or something like that.

Here are the VRPs in Jerusalem, remembering that Cornelius is one of the good ones, and saying, "Cool."

Behold! Acts 11, 12, 13, 14.

Here is Paul, formerly known as Saul, coming out of hiding in Tarsus (Acts 11:25–26) to finally help the church he now loves. Here are Paul and Barnabas, traveling far and wide with the good news of God's reign on their lips. Here are many who won't/can't/don't think Jesus is the Messiah they need; here are many more who will/can/do. Here are Gentiles, many more Gentiles, oodles and oodles of Gentiles, saying yes to God getting everything God wants. It turns out, they want that too. Baptisms galore. Not just of the good ones—of anyone who asks.

Behold! Acts 15.

Here are the VRPs back in Jerusalem, hearing about the giant Gentile party Paul is throwing. Here are the VRPs' emissaries, traveling north to Antioch to see if it's true. It is true. Here are Paul and Barnabas defending, debating, insisting. Here is an invitation for them to come to Jerusalem and take it up with the VRPs themselves. It's not really an invitation.

(Here are Paul and Barnabas campaigning, telling all the Christians along the way what great things God has done with all those Gentiles [Acts 15:3]. Here is Paul, with whom you really do not want to get into an argument, because you will lose.)

Here is the crux of the Jerusalem VRPs' argument: Gentiles can be Jesus people, sure, but they have to convert to Judaism first—circumcision, Torah keeping, the whole nine yards. Everybody knows it's true.

Here is the surprising reality to me, a Gentile: *they're not wrong.* Here is their Bible saying they're right. Here is the Bible saying it a lot of times: God does not favor Gentiles. God doesn't even like Gentiles. God has often called for Gentiles to be wiped off the map.

Here is Deuteronomy 7, for one. Try to read it without it upsetting your stomach. Here is Isaiah 40, not just the part we read at Advent, but a little further down the page:

> All the nations are as nothing before [God];
> they are accounted by [God] as less than nothing and
> emptiness. (Isa. 40:17)

Here are the VRPs, and they know what the scriptures say. They know what their ancestors told them. They even know what Jesus said, though it is not yet in scripture:

> These twelve Jesus sent out with the following instructions: "Go nowhere among the Gentiles, and enter no town of the Samaritans, but go rather to the lost sheep of the house of Israel. As you go, proclaim the good news, 'The kingdom of heaven has come near.'" (Matt. 10:5–7)

Here they are, not wrong, the Jerusalem, Jesus-loving VRPs who think Gentiles *could* be admitted into the reign of God, if they would first become less Gentile, change their identity, endure a round of conversion therapy.

Here is Peter, telling his story again, only this time he skips the sheet and the voice and the travel and gets right to the point: "And God, who knows the human heart, testified to them by giving them the Holy Spirit, just as [God] did to us" (Acts 15:8).

Here are Barnabas and Paul, telling similar stories, oodles and oodles of stories, about the surprise collision of the Holy Spirit with Gentiles everywhere they've traveled. Here are the VRPs keeping very quiet, listening, feeling the earth shift on its axis, feeling their very own DNA uncoil and recoil in the opposite direction, feeling the world turn inside out. *Here is the Spirit of the living Christ, in Gentiles. Huh. Imagine that. Here we are, imagining that.*

Here is James the Elder, standing up. Here is James, digging deep into his Sabbath school memory bank to recall Amos, an ancient Hebrew Bible prophet, the oldest of the old. Here is James, saying what we already know to be true: "Our Bible says more than one thing about all this." Here is James, shifting the axis, bending the arc: "Mostly it says God does not include Gentiles in God's covenant with us. But sometimes it says—" And then James quotes from the Prophets:

> "After this I will return, and I will rebuild the dwelling of David, which has fallen; from its ruins I will rebuild it, and I will set it up, so that *all other peoples* may seek the Lord—*even all the Gentiles* over whom my name has been called. Thus says the Lord, who has been making these things known from long ago." (Acts 15:15-18, emphasis mine, but probably also James's, don't you think?)

Here is James, finding that new experiences of God's presence and power in the world call for new readings of old scriptures. Here is the Bible, giving up a minority report that no reader could see until they had to. Here is the church, figuring it out, learning something new about the God they thought they already knew. Here are Paul and Barnabas, headed back to Antioch clutching a letter in their fists, a letter that says the Gentiles are in.

Here is the best line from that letter:

> For it has seemed good to the Holy Spirit and to us to impose on you no further burden than these essentials. (Acts 15:28)

Here is God, drawing people into partnership. *It has seemed good to the Holy Spirit and to us* . . . Here is God, not bullying or coercing or commanding or threatening, but inviting. *It has seemed good to the Holy Spirit and to us* . . . Here are God's people, saying yes. *It has seemed good to the Holy Spirit and to us.* Here are God's people, caring.

Here is God, getting everything God wants.

Behold.*

Something, Something, Holy Spirit

That story unfolding over six chapters in Acts helps me remember to be grateful. Because the OG Christians decided to let me in, it has first-order importance for my own faith. It's because it "seemed good to the Holy Spirit and to [them]" that the Gentile knee I was dandled on was a Christian one.

But—and!—the story has second-order importance for the way it demonstrates what to do when everything you think you know about scripture (and thus about God) doesn't line up with what you are experiencing IRL, particularly when you suspect the Holy Spirit might be at work where you thought she couldn't/wouldn't/ didn't. As a good fundagelical, I learned that the Bible said every- thing I needed to know about how the world works, and everything in my world that did not conform would have to be reconsidered, realigned, or rejected.

But in Acts 10–15 the Bible itself shows us that sometimes, in the special case of unmistakable Holy Spirit activity, we're called on to read the Bible anew, with new eyes to see what is there to be seen. We're called to be like James the Elder reading (or recalling) Amos, finding there the minority report that helped him see the inclusion of the Gentiles in God's heart all along. Yes, it's meta: the Bible in- cluding a story about rereading and reinterpreting the Bible.**

---

* For this reading of Acts 10–15, and for my conviction that this section of scrip- ture is central to the church's understanding of how experiences of God in sur- prising places (people) send us back to the Bible to look for a minority report, I am entirely indebted to Luke Timothy Johnson's *Scripture and Discernment: Decision Making in the Church* (1983). Seriously. That book changed everything for me, and now I tell the Acts 10–15 story every chance I get. Thank you for coming to my TED talk.

** Well actually, there are lots of stories in the Bible about reading the Bible.

The story leads us to ask:

Is the Bible a book that reveals all we need to know about God; everything God intends to show us about this world; the complete, consistent, culture-free set of knowledge and understanding required to live a good and godly life, world without end, amen, amen?*

Or

Is the Bible an overstuffed, super messy filing cabinet of reports from all kinds of people over dozens of generations with all kinds of perspectives who, in their day, responded the best they could (some of them better, some of them worse) to a God who is hard to pin down but always invitational, always asking people to try or do or see or believe or *be* something altogether new—written and preserved for our sake, so that people in every age can better recognize what God is doing the next time we see God at work, so that it (the Bible) must be taken with utmost seriousness?**

Another way of asking, because all our questions about the Bible are really, underneath, questions about God:

Is it necessary for the holding together of your Christian faith that God's own self remains precisely the same yesterday, today, and

---

Israelites in exile found scrolls no one had seen for generations, and thereby renewed their faith; Jesus read the Bible and reinterpreted it in the hearing of disciples, crowds, and enemies; Peter clarified the Pentecostal chaos of Acts 2 by recalling Joel from the Hebrew Bible; the Egyptian queen's treasurer from Acts 8 found in Isaiah 53 a suffering servant much like himself, "cut off" and "stricken," and asked if Jesus could be his Lord too. There are many more, and they often demonstrate the necessity of rereading and rehearing old scriptures for new lives in new times and places.

* Sometimes people use code words to get at this idea. They say the Bible is "inerrant" or "infallible," or they say it's necessary to take the Bible "literally." I suppose if you think it's complete, consistent, and culture-free, that could work.

** Perhaps you're aware that Karl Barth, an important systematic theologian of the twentieth century, when asked if he took the Bible literally, said, "No, I take the Bible far too seriously to take it literally." You don't even have to like Barth to appreciate the value of that distinction.

forever, so that our apprehension of God and God's ways must be cut from the exact same cloth as, say, Peter's? or Paul's?

Or

Is it possible that God has been inviting people into new under-standings of God—where God is, what God does, who God loves—for as long as people have been telling stories about God, and that the Bible testifies to the truth of that, and invites us to look for God everywhere, recognize God wherever we can, even if we find God in places (people) that are guaranteed to disrupt what we already think we know for sure?

At Galileo Church we've developed a kind of shorthand for talking about something that happens with delightful regularity in our life together. The formula works like this:

1. We have a problem we don't know how to fix. Usually it's a prob-lem about people, and power, and sharing—the really sticky stuff, I'm talking about.

2. We take multiple swings at solving it and miss every time. There's no shame in a swing and a miss, but it's vexing.

3. A sudden solution comes from an unexpected corner (quiet per-son, new person, young person, cranky person, neurodiverse person, two or three or four unrelated people get the same idea at the same time, etc.). Said solution disrupts the status quo, pushes us beyond the boundaries of reason, turns the situation upside down, and is obviously and hilariously the right way to go.

4. We celebrate by retelling 1 through 3, always ending with, "And then . . . [*shrug*] . . . *something, something, Holy Spirit.*" High fives all around. If the Holy Spirit had hands, we would high-five her too.

"Something, something, Holy Spirit" is the best way we know how to give credit where it's due—to the God of the universe who keeps showing up, especially by giving us ideas that we're pretty dang sure we didn't generate by our own brainpower. Our brainpower, after all, is allocated according to evolutionary biology, dedicated to our own survival and the survival of our descendants. Our brains work for us, to get us more of what we want. But the Spirit in us reroutes our energies toward what God wants. It's how we imagine our biblical ancestors telling their own stories:

> Hagar remembers, "After they threw us out, I carried my boy on my back till our canteen ran dry. Honestly, we were just wandering in circles. I had no idea where we could go. Finally I set him down under a tree, kissed his sweaty head while I took my last deep breaths of him; he smelled like everything I ever loved in this world. I went to sit under a different tree—I didn't wanna see what was coming for both of us—and that's when, well, *something, something, water well,* and I knew we were gonna be OK." (Gen. 21:8-21)

> Jacob laughs about it now: "So I'm on the run from Esau, cuz he was definitely gonna kill me if he caught me, and I'm not saying I didn't deserve it. But I have to sleep sometime, so I lay my head on a rock, say a little prayer to whichever deity is in charge of that place. Just a shout-out, all due respect, right? But while I'm asleep, *something, something, angel ladder,* and when I wake up, I just know: God is God here too. God is God everywhere. And I say to myself, 'Self, I think you're gonna be OK.'" (Gen. 28:10-17)

> Moses shrugs, "I just figured I'd work my father-in-law's sheep till he died and they became my sheep. I wasn't real ambitious; I'm a simple man with simple needs. Then one day—I know you know, I've told it a million times—*something, something, burning bush*—and here I am, liberating my kin from their oppressor with nothing but a staff and a smile. And oh yeah, Aaron and Miriam, they helped too." (Exodus)

> The Israelites told the same story to their kids over and over again: "Worked our fingers to the bone, and what did we get? Bony fingers. Then one day Moses comes back around, gets into it with Pharaoh. Next thing you know, *something, something, locusts; something, something, frogs; something, something, hail; yada yada yada; something, something, angel of death.* Who knew there was an angel of death? Anyway, *boom!* Here we are, learning how to stop working and take a nap every seven days. Whole new life." (also Exodus)

> Everybody Jesus ever met had a story to tell. "They said it was glaucoma; my grandma had it too. It kept getting worse until I couldn't see, couldn't work. I couldn't even move, I was so afraid of crashing into stuff. Then this guy comes to town. I don't know who he was. He says to me, 'Here's mud in your eye.' And *something, something, 'twas blind but now I see.* That's really all I know. Don't ask me any more." (John 9)

> The OG Christians, late at night after several shared skins of cheap fruit of the vine, would shake their heads remembering how it went down: "It all happened so *fast!* We thought we'd have more time, do some strategic planning, develop some policies, maybe hire a consultant, get used to the water, right? But every time we turned around, *something, something, Holy Spirit*— and there she was, pushing new people in the door, shoving new people into the deep end like she knew they could swim, saying yes to way more people than we thought she should. She worked *fast.* I mean, we're glad they all came; we're like family now. But. It was just so . . . *fast."* (Acts 10–15)

Something, something, Holy Spirit. It's a useful formula; it keeps us from having to explain what can't always be explained. Explaining how God showed up—what it looked like, sounded like, smelled like, felt like—tends to dry it out somehow, wringing all the mystery out of it. It's the worst kind of humansplaining. It's like ruining a joke by saying why it's funny.

And what I'm saying is, "something, something, Holy Spirit" keeps on happening. God keeps on showing up. The Spirit of the living Christ puts in appearances, presses her case by giving abundant gifts to unexpected people, hoping (in God's chronic naivete) that humanity will *catch on*, for crying out loud.

Yes, beyond the pages of the Bible, I'm saying. Unto this very day, and beyond.

8

CATCHING ON, CATCHING UP

You know how some movies are teed up for a sequel in the final scene, and as the credits roll you find yourself anticipating how much fun it will be to catch up with characters whose arc clearly has a distance yet to travel? Or how some books cry out for another installment with an updated setting and better cellphones? The Bible is like that: there are plotlines begun within its pages that aren't really wrapped up by the canon's closure.

That is to say, there are things God starts in the pages of scripture that God hasn't yet finished within the pages of scripture. That whole conflict between Jewish Christians and Gentile Christians, for example, doesn't actually get all the way resolved with James the Elder's announcement in Acts 15. We can see that one playing out in Paul's epistles to the churches he started, where the ongoing theological rift has the potential to become interpersonally contentious* and to damage the church's loving reputation.

But the ethnic division between Jesus's followers was far from the only manifestation of the fragmentation of the human family

---

* See especially the epistle to the Galatians, where Paul tells his side of the story, including the harassment of new converts by some who still advocated for strict adherence to Torah as a sign of respect for the Jewish origins of Christian faith, and reports his disappointment and frustration with Peter's unwillingness to stand up to the bullies by sitting down to dinner (and probably the Eucharist) with the whole church (Gal. 2:11–14).

playing out in our ancestors' culture and church. The generalized instruction throughout the Bible to "love your neighbor" required specific correctives along the way to help them (us) see that the better part of love requires liberation from the power differentials that keep some people up and some people down, or hold some people in while forcing some people out.

And in several cases, the prescriptions for resolving the imbalance are like arrows launched from a bow—the arrow is launched in the Bible's pages, but it has not landed by the time you turn the last page.* Our ancestors in faith could point to possibilities for equity and equilibrium as features of God getting everything God wants, but they hadn't achieved those aims just yet.

They were waiting, as it turns out, for it to seem good to the Holy Spirit and to . . . us. Yep, that's right—a couple thousand years down the road, some arrows launched by our ancestors in faith are finally landing. Here are three cases where I've seen it.

Enslavement

Case #1: White Christians' support and perpetration of the enslavement of Black bodies in the United States and Europe for a shamefully long damn time.

White Christians were distressingly slow to recognize that the enslavement of Black bodies made a lie of the white church's faith. And why couldn't they see it for so long? Because the Bible reports that our ancestors in faith enslaved people, sometimes, and were themselves enslaved, sometimes. The Bible gives instructions for the Christian comportment of both enslaved persons and their enslavers. And, let's face it, it was in white Christians' own self-

---

* Like James the Elder reading Amos the prophet in Acts 15. Amos let the arrow of Gentile inclusion fly, but it didn't land until Peter and Paul gave their testimony in Jerusalem and the VRPs of the early church said yes to Cornelius and the rest of humanity.

interest to believe that the majority report in the Bible was all they needed to hear about that. White Christians believed they had a *biblical* warrant for owning other people, so they did it for a couple hundred years without compunction or conscience.

It would be a long damn time after the biblical canon's closure, centuries after enslaved people were exhorted to "obey [their] earthly lords with fear and trembling," and slaveholders reminded to "stop threatening [the enslaved], for you . . . both have the same Lord in heaven" (Eph. 6:5-9, with my modifications to the translation), before mainstream, white Christianity stopped using such texts to justify enslavement for white Christians' own economic gain. *

I have to imagine that, at some point, white Christians somewhere recognized the presence of the Spirit of the living Christ in Black persons, Black families, Black community; recognized that the *imago Dei* (image of God) comes to life in unending varieties of human bodies; recognized that the Bible itself says more than one thing about slavery. ** The Bible includes a minority report, one that can be seen when readers become aware that the Holy Spirit is doing something other than what the majority report taught them to expect.

The Bible includes the little epistle of Philemon, for example, in which Paul the Apostle asks a wealthy slaveholder (that's Phi-

---

* White Christians have been distressingly and infuriatingly slow too to recognize that Christian faith calls for repentance and repair of the great sin of slavery (even before reconciliation)—not just the recognition of civil rights for people of color, but a civil reckoning for the privilege whiteness still affords in this country and this culture.

** I'm writing from a white person's perspective about the recognition and repentance that would be necessary for white Christians to reject slavery as a valid economic arrangement for Christian households or businesses, and to actively seek to dismantle systems of enslavement in their own contexts and around the world. Not because the rightness or wrongness of anything depends on white people's recognition of it, but because the issue here is the dismantling of a power structure by the people who benefit from it.

lemon) to think of Onesimus, an enslaved person, as a brother in Christ rather than as property. This would carry instructions such as the one in Ephesians 5:9 ("for you . . . both have the same Lord in heaven") to their logical end. Paul suggests to Philemon in a brilliant piece of rhetoric that Christian siblinghood would not only allow but necessitate the liberation of the one man by the other.

The epistle is not an Emancipation Proclamation, by a long shot, but it aims in that direction. It opens the possibility for the windy Holy Spirit to propel Philemon, along with the church in his house, into a new understanding of Onesimus's humanity—like Peter recognizing something new about Cornelius the Gentile. And Philemon's potential response to this new understanding allows subsequent readers of his correspondence from Paul to imagine a new possibility: no enslavement, no buying and selling of human beings as commodities, as this is very much *not* what God wants.

Philemon, I'm saying (the epistle, not the dude), is representative of a quiet but provocative minority report in the Bible regarding slavery. Yes, our ancestors in faith were both slaveholders and enslaved persons, and they could be counted as God's people either way. But our slaveholding ancestors were not yet in full partnership with God getting everything God wants. Not yet—but their stories in the Bible opened up, rather than closed down, the possibility for us to consider something new with respect to the rights and dignity of all human beings. The Bible never told white Christian slaveholders to free the people they enslaved—but the Holy Spirit did.

It took an underground railroad, slave revolts, abolitionist activists, a civil war, a presidential proclamation, and—*something, something, Holy Spirit*—to dismantle the evil economic system of slavery in this country. God knows we are miles away from real justice with respect to race in these United States, as well as in the church and in the hearts of white Christians, myself included. There are even some remaining who would stand on the Bible as justification for racist ideology. But where we have seen the moral universe's arc bending, we know how to tell the story: *Something, something, Holy Spirit; God gets everything God wants.*

Patriarchy

Case #2: Church-enforced, Bible-justified patriarchy. *

Biblical patriarchy perpetuated a system by which girls and women were counted as the property of their fathers, then husbands, and were assumed to have little capacity to learn, discern, earn, teach, plan, lead, dissent, protest, or otherwise contribute to and benefit from decision-making in their household, society, or (especially) their church.

This hierarchy with men at the tippy-top of the church's power structures stayed in place long past the point of culture's rigorous reinforcement of such. "Because the Bible says so" was the usual answer from the men and women I asked, when I was a little girl, why it should be that my full personhood would never be recognized in the church I loved so deeply.

They were not wrong. Our (male) biblical ancestors subscribed to patriarchy and inscribed it in practically every verse of scripture. I worked for years to exegete** away the New Testament's endorsement of patriarchy, hoping to uncover the equity I longed for. It didn't work, exactly. Sometimes the apparent misogyny could be cleared up with a quick vocabulary check; other times I did handstands with the text to soften its edges and flatten its hierarchy. My own mother said at one point, "If it's that hard to make your case,

---

* Patriarchy and misogyny, I should say, though it's hard to say which comes first and causes the other. It's kind of a chicken-and-egg situation with those two. At The Gathering, a womanist church in Dallas, my colleagues Rev. Dr. Irie Session and Rev. Kamilah Hall Sharp call for dismantling PMS: patriarchy, misogyny, and sexism, all rolled up together.

** "Exegete"—a method of carefully examining the vocabulary, syntax, and context of scripture in its original language, with the aim of achieving clarity about what it meant when it was written.

perhaps it's not a good case."* I ended up with a confusing jumble of verses, and the same old swirl of conflicting ideas about what it means to be a woman in the household of God.

Only recently have feminist and womanist readers recovered the reality of the giftedness of girls and women all along the way in the Bible's story of God, the universe, and everything. These readers have uncovered a strong minority report throughout, showing God's people catching on to new understandings of what God can do, will do, and has done in the lives of women.

Take, for example, the daughters of Zelophehad.** In the Hebrew Bible book of Numbers, when the (male) descendants of liberated (male) Israelites were counted in a census and allotted property in the land they would soon occupy, Z's daughters protested (Num. 27). Their father had died in the forty-year wandering. They had no brothers. They were as yet unmarried. According to the patriarchal census, they would receive no share of property.

Moses heard their protest, brought their case to God (!), and God said, "You know, I think they're right. Here's what we'll do." Then *something, something, Holy Spirit*, and Z's daughters got their property, and their case became precedent for other women who would find themselves unattached to men when it came time for property to be passed down to the next generation. It was not the true equity women would come to enjoy a few millennia later—it was still as-

---

* My mother is one of the strongest women I know, and fully on board with the biblical-theological necessity of equity for women and men in the church *now*. But back then it was harder, because we both still thought we had to find every answer about what God wants expressed with complete clarity within the pages of the Bible.

** What?! You haven't heard of them? Take up *Badass Women of the Bible: Inspiration from Biblical Women Who Challenged and Subverted Patriarchy* (2019) by the Rev. Dr. Irie Session. The badass daughters of Zelophehad get a whole chapter. Enjoy also Wilda Gafney's *Womanist Midrash: A Reintroduction to the Women of the Torah and the Throne* (2017), where Z's daughters are also in the spotlight.

sumed that a woman held property only so long as there was no related man to obviate her claim—but if we're listening closely, we can hear the Spirit whispering a new idea. It sounds kinda like an arrow whistling as it flies through the air.

When the whole, capable, Spirit-filled humanity of women can be seen in scripture, the church's eyes can be opened enough to see capable, Spirit-filled women in the church, even if the Bible clearly says lots of times that women shouldn't/can't/don't count as much as men. Or, sometimes, when the church's eyes are open enough to see the capable, Spirit-filled women who are right there in the middle of them, the church can suddenly see all the remarkable instances of capable, Spirit-filled women in the Bible. It works both ways. Chicken and egg in a whole new way.

Just as importantly, the church that sees past the patriarchy of the Bible into the new, equitable possibility the Holy Spirit makes visible starts to see something else: the women all around them who can't or won't be part of the church as long as their whole humanity is obscured by patriarchy.

The problem of patriarchy persists in many churches, of course, and the Bible's noisy majority makes it hard to hear the minority voices of Mahlah, Tirzah, Hoglah, Milcah, and Noah (yeah, Z's daughters had names; they were a pretty big deal). But where Christian eyes and hearts are open, we can see that the Holy Spirit keeps showing up, bending that arc, making new things happen. *Something, something, Holy Spirit; God gets everything God wants.*

Interlude: Paul the Apostle and Paul the Prophet

In all of our talk about the ancient prophets of both the Hebrew Bible and the New Testament, we haven't yet mentioned Paul. His appearances in this book have been in his role as an apostle: from his Acts 10-15 fame converting oodles and oodles of Gentiles as the evangelistic partner of Barnabas, and as a correspondent with Philemon.

It's also important to know that during his apostolic travels he became the church's first theologian. Paul is the guy who thought through the implications of Jesus's messiahship, not just for his own (and Jesus's) kin, but for all the people of the world, and indeed for the world itself, the very earth of which we are made (see Rom. 8:19–23, e.g.).

We know Paul, too, as the church's first ethicist. It's Paul who worked out so many instances of what it looks like, here and now, for God to get everything God wants.

> It looks like people waiting for each other at the Lord's table, making sure everyone gets enough to eat (1 Cor. 11:20–22).
> It looks like the giftedness-by-the-Holy-Spirit of every person being the singular assessment for their appropriate role in the church family (Rom. 12, 1 Cor. 12, Eph. 4).
> It looks like dividing walls between different kinds of humans being torn down as we learn to live together in the church (Eph. 2).
> It looks like people sacrificing status for the sake of unity among believers (Phil. 2).
> It looks like stronger people helping weaker people however they can (Rom. 14, 1 Cor. 8).
> It looks like hope and comfort for the grieving that is endemic to human life (1 Thess. 4).
> It looks like purity of heart and self-controlled action, so that the proclivities of the individual will do no harm to the beloved community (also 1 Thess. 4).[*]

---

[*] As with Barth, you could not like Paul very much and still be wowed by his kick-ass theological mind. Without him (Paul), we might be left with Jesus-the-Really-Good-Guy-of-the-Gospels, wow. With him, we get Jesus-the-Savior-of-the-World, *wow!* Yep, Paul might have been sexist, at least a little homophobic, and weirdly repressed. But like our grandmas, he's a swirl of good and not-so-good. Like our grandmas, he's completely redeemable. Even lovable. If you try.

But Paul wasn't concerned only with Christian comportment here and now. It turns out that all his ideas about what God wants in the present came from his ideas about what God wants *ultimately*. Like all biblical and contemporary prophets, he could see, somehow, God getting everything God wants, even when it was clearly not happening yet. He could see that

> in Christ Jesus you are all children of God through faith. As many of you as were baptized into Christ have clothed your- selves with Christ. There is no longer Jew or Greek, there is no longer slave or free, there is no longer male and female; for all of you are one in Christ Jesus. And if you belong to Christ, then you are Abraham's offspring, heirs according to the promise. (Gal. 3:26–29)

This was Paul's vision: divisions between people disappear "in Christ." First, the ethnic distinction that threatened to tear apart the early church: "no longer Jew or Greek" (Greek being another way to say "Gentile"—i.e., everybody who's not Jewish). Then, the eco- nomic distinction that preserved a nasty power dynamic between people: "no longer slave or free." Finally, the patriarchy/misogyny that established hierarchy according to the allotment of chromo- somes: "no longer male and female."

"In Christ," Paul says, it becomes possible for us to look out for each other's interests, because we no longer imagine that we have to protect our own advantage—because there is no advantage to pro- tect! All humanity is invited into Abraham (and Sarah's) family tree, written into their will, eligible to inherit everything God ever promised to our ancestors in faith, irrespective of any human-made and human-enforced hierarchy of persons.

It might go without saying, but I'll say it anyway: this vision of flattening hierarchy could not have been more different than the Roman Empire's idea of how to keep control of all its conquered lands. Empire loves hierarchy and thrives by keeping everyone in their right place. Roman citizens versus their conquerees . . . land-owners/slaveholders versus working class / enslaved workers . . . men with rights afforded by empire versus women toiling without a voice—this is how the world worked then and there.

And don't get me started on the here and now. Those racial/economic/gender differences are easily activated, setting us against each other, all of us afraid to lose whatever power we think we've got. Cynical leaders pit citizens against immigrants, white people against BIPOC, wealthy suburbanites against the urban poor, het-cis family values against queer identity . . . it has ever been thus.

For Paul to envision all of those "versuses" floating away in the baptismal waters—well, you'd have to be a prophet to see something like that. A prophet with a strong dose of *something, something, Holy Spirit.*

Now here's where all this is going.

Queer Exclusion

Case #3: The exclusion of LGBTQ+ persons from the life and leadership of the Christian church.

Maybe you already know that at Galileo Church we celebrate and activate the inclusion of all people in God's family, including and especially LGBTQ+ persons. Maybe you wonder how or why we do that, since you know full well that the Bible says being gay is not OK.

Or maybe now you're catching on, after we've done so much work together. You know the Bible *also* says Gentiles are gross and God doesn't like them. You know the Bible *also* says it's OK with God for white people to buy and sell Black bodies. You know the Bible *also* says God thinks gender-based hierarchy is nifty and has lots of ideas to help us do it better. So the simplistic "the Bible says being gay is not OK" argument isn't going to work all that well anymore, is it?

I could spend some pages here explaining why I think it's really iffy that the Bible says anything at all about contemporary queerness. Yes, there is a sprinkling of passages that seem to say that having sex with someone of your own sex is not good. We could run through them sometime, if you like, one at a time. It does not take long, as there are not many. It's not that hard to show that they don't actually address gay or lesbian (or other nonstraight) orientation, especially since there's no vocabulary for sexual orientation of any kind, including straightness, in the ancient languages of the Bible. *

But. My argument here in no way depends on proving that the Bible is not homophobic or transphobic, or even just infuriatingly cis-heteronormative. After all, big chunks of the Bible are racist, classist, sexist . . . but we think our churches should not be any of those things, because the Spirit of the living Christ has shown us differently, right? Right.

The thing I know now that I did not always know is this: homophobia and transphobia, or even a gentler form of exclusion or diminishment of LGBTQ+ persons ("love the sinner, hate the sin," *blech*), make a lie of my Christian faith. There is no more room in the church for excluding queer believers (or queer questioners, for that matter) than for enslaving people to clean up after our potlucks, or excluding ethnic groups we think of as lesser than ourselves, or keeping women from ordination or any other role for which they are gifted. All of which the Bible would allow, right? If the Bible were all we had to go on?

What I'm saying is, the Bible is *not* all we have to go on. The Spirit of the living Christ keeps working, and arrows that were launched within the pages of the Bible keep flying—toward inclusion and embrace, toward repentance for our previous misunder-

* I have written a little book about that, actually; it's called *For the Bible Tells Me So: The Biblical-Theological Case for LGBTQ+ Inclusion in the Church* (2020). It includes a bibliography of even more books about how the Bible doesn't say what you might have been told it says about being queer.

standing of the Spirit's intent, toward dissolution of division and one reconciled humanity. The arrows fly toward God getting everything God wants.

Were I to explain exhaustively and comprehensively all the reasons why the church I founded is queer-inclusive all the way down, the world itself could not contain the books that would be written. But from what I've already written here, perhaps you can resonate with these reasons, at least:

> › Because prophetic visions of God's beautiful future are inclusive of "all peoples," "all nations," "the good and the bad"—in other words, *everybody*.

> › Because the arc of the moral universe is long, but it bends toward justice, toward love in public, where every human being is loved and valued for their whole personhood.

> › Because Jesus spent the entirety of his ministry defying religious law and cultural propriety by hanging out with people on the margins, saying in every way he knew how that the reign of God is especially good news for the kicked out and the left out, for the small and underappreciated.

> › Because God is the kind of God who is always, always, always calling people into new understandings of where God is and what God does and who God loves.

> › Because the Acts 8 eunuch reading Isaiah 53 found himself in the pages of scripture, and then found himself again in Isaiah 56:3–8, and Philip baptized him into the family of God on the spot, without objection from anyone. And I'm not saying the eunuch was "gay" or "trans"—those categories don't make any sense in the context of our biblical ancestors—but I'm awfully certain he was *not* straight, *not* cisgender, but something else, something extraordinary, something quite *queer*; and also a beloved, baptized child of the God who made him, with whom God was so pleased.

> Because the church has been called on again and again to re-think who is "in" and who is "out," always resolving in the in-clusion of those who were previous excluded, or the elevation of those who were previously diminished.

> Because the Bible says more than one thing about gender and sexuality, some things loudly and insistently, some things more quietly but equally insistently.

> Because in Christ there is no male and female.

> Because the Bible shows us again and again *in its own pages* that it is meant to be reread and reinterpreted when the Spirit shows up and does something unexpected and otherwise inexplicable.

> Because Cornelius and his Gentile household got the Spirit, hallelujah!

> Because, like Peter at Cornelius's house, I have seen the Holy Spirit in LGBTQ+ persons. Or I should say, I have seen gifts in queer people that I cannot attribute to any other source. In my queer siblings in Christ I have seen love, joy, peace, and pa-tience; I have seen kindness, gentleness, faithfulness, gener-osity, and self-control. These are the fruit of the Spirit of the living Christ. Against such there is no law. [*]

> Because, then, if God gave them the same gift(s) God gave us (cisgender, straight folx) when we believed in the Lord Jesus Christ, who are we that we could hinder God? [**]

> Because Jesus has abolished the law with its commandments and ordinances, that he might create in himself one new hu-manity in place of the two, thus making peace, and might rec-oncile both groups to God in one body through the cross. [***] Why would I spend one joule of energy doing anything other than celebrating the one new humanity, leaning into it, using

---

[*] Gal. 5:22–23.

[**] Acts 10:17, paraphrased.

[***] Eph. 2:15–16.

all the energy I've got to make it more true *here* and *now*, this lovely vision of God's lovely future?

> *Because God gets everything God wants.*

Well. Now I've gone to preaching.

Conclusion

I'm not going to tell you that I've solved the problem of the miserable, overcrowded Moria refugee camp burning down and redisplacing thousands of already displaced people during a global pandemic. In my own prayers and in my own heart, God is not off the hook for the suffering of those bodies and souls.

But I cannot get around this true thing about God: that God has not let *us* off the hook for that, either. God wants buy-in from us, wants us to *catch on*, wants us to get a glimpse of where this cosmic train is headed and to *get on board*. God has given us lots of not-so-subtle hints, about both how this world is supposed to work and how far we are from that. The invitation to partnership starts to sound urgent, doesn't it? Like an invitation to a wedding banquet we best not turn down. I think God is probably justified in thinking we should know by now what to do in response to that Afghan man's indictment of humanity, "Nobody care, nobody care."

Which then turns into the question of our lifetime: given all that we've seen and heard, what are we to do?

Or: what does the Christian life look like, here and now, if God ultimately gets everything God wants, *and* God is not yet, not always, getting everything God wants?

PART FOUR

I WANT TO WANT WHAT GOD WANTS

9

ONE THING GOD WANTS IS YOU

So here we are: God has a dream, the long arc of the moral universe is bending toward God's dream, we (the human family) have been called into partnership in the bending of it, and God seems willing to wait for us to step up so that we can say, along the way, "It has seemed good to the Holy Spirit and to us . . ."

Here, then, is one way to sum up the Whole Human Project, the Everything-I-Am-Meant-to-Be-and-Do-with-My-One-Wild-and-Precious-Life:

I want what God wants.

Do I Want What God Wants?

OK, more accurately, I want to want what God wants.

Because I have to confess that I don't *always* want what God wants. See, I was born pretty near the tippy-top of Privilege Mountain. I'm white, North American, cisgender, straight, and Christian.* When God's prophets speak about God's cosmic remodeling, they seem to think my mountain will be leveled as other people's

---

* Being dandled on a Christian knee is indeed a piece of privilege in the United States, where a Christian majority can incite Islamophobia, for example, with impunity. What percentage of governors, senators, congresspeople, Supreme Court justices, presidents, high-ranking military officers, university presidents, and Fortune 500 executives are Christian? Think about it.

valleys of oppression are filled in. I stand to lose quite a bit when the arc of the moral universe finally hits its mark. So I pray my confession: "God, I *want* to want what you want." And I ask for the renovation of my own desires.

If God gets everything God wants, and if we trust that it could feel like heaven for us when that happens, then learning what God wants and conforming our own wanting to what God wants becomes the basis for our one wild and precious life* lived in faith.

At Galileo Church we've found that wanting what God wants gets us real leverage for imagining and embodying full-throated worship, life-giving ethics, risky truth-telling, subversive economics, patient activism, mutually satisfying relationships, nonconsumeristic beauty, and so much more. We can derive pretty much everything we need for Christian living by locating ourselves within these two questions we're always asking of ourselves and each other:

1. What does God want?
2. What does it look like for us to want (and work for and receive and cooperate with and celebrate) more of *that*?

God Wants (All of) You: Beautiful, Broken, Burdened

Answer #1 to the question "What does God want?": God wants all of you (and everybody else).

When it comes to you (and everybody else), I have a bad habit that I should own up to. It's akin to that thing Enneagram aficionados do, when they secretly decide they know *your* number even if you don't know your number and don't want to know theirs either. (They tell me there's a number for people like me.)

---

* From the poem by Mary Oliver, "The Summer Day." I know you know it. Take a break from this book; go read it again.

Here's my comparable foible: I tend to think I know, after talking to you for a few minutes, whether your own self-assessment is "I'm beautiful," "I'm broken," or "I'm burdened." At least, in terms of Christian theology, I have a pretty good idea which assessment of the human family you inherited from the church of your youth or from your family of origin or from wherever you learned your anthropology—that is to say, wherever you learned what human beings are like, and thus what *you* are like.

"I'm beautiful" people start at the very beginning, when God made human beings in God's own image in Genesis 1 and declared them the pinnacle of the created order, the crowning achievement of everything that God assessed as "very good" (Gen. 1:31). "I'm beautiful" people are secure in their own identity and trust their experiences of the world. They wish the same for everyone else. They believe they know the right thing to do and say much of the time, and they rarely question their own motives. Mistakes don't feel catastrophic; they happen to everyone and can be learning experiences for the future. "I'm beautiful" people rely on strong self-care to bring themselves back to their certainty of God's love for them—and their equal certainty that they cannot love anyone else if they do not first love themselves well and truly.

"I'm broken" people think Genesis 1 was a terrific start, but Genesis 3 is more instructive for the lived human experience. One transgression by our originary ancestors reveals that we are at root self-interested, self-deceived, and self-destructive. "I'm broken" people know this in their bones, and they are not afraid to admit it. They can face the truth that their own motives, even for good and generous actions, are often corrupt. They are in touch with their own hankerings, their tendency to take more than their fair share, their lack of trust in other people. Indeed, how can they trust anyone, if brokenness is definitional of the human condition? More than anything, "I'm broken" people seek forgiveness and understanding from self, from other people, and from God.

"I'm burdened" people are acutely aware of the brokenness of All Things in Genesis 3—not just the brokenness of individual persons, but of the earth itself. The originary brokenness affects whole systems, visible and invisible powers that be, such that power is unevenly and dangerously distributed throughout the human family. Those with less power (fewer resources, lower status, worse luck) are weighted down by the brokenness of those above them on the ladder of human hierarchy. "I'm burdened" people see clearly that prejudice keeps some people down and privilege keeps some people up; the system is rigged, and personal virtue is hardly helpful in repairing it. Righteous anger can be effective, on one's own behalf or on behalf of people who are similarly burdened; or it can just be exhausting. "I'm burdened" people hunger and thirst for justice and rest.

Please feel free to be as annoyed by those paragraphs as you want. It's so silly to categorize people broadly this way. But at least let me defend myself by saying that I wrote each of those profiles based on someone I know quite well; in each case I held the person lovingly in my mind and described what I know of their inner life as truthfully as I could. I should probably also say that in each case— beautiful, broken, and burdened—the model was me.

Surprise! Betcha didn't see that one coming.

Or maybe you did. Because maybe you were already finding some of yourself in each of the three descriptions. Maybe if you read these pages on a Monday morning you'd resonate more with "beautiful." Maybe if you read them on a Thursday afternoon you'd get more hits with "broken." Maybe if you read them in particular seasons in your life or in the life of the world, "burdened" would be the only one that makes any sense at all.

What I'm saying, harking back to that ice cream swirl of a grandma we've all got, is that human beings are complicated mixtures of the good, the bad, and the ugly.* And you knew that al-

---

* The good, the bad, and the ugly—those just might correspond to "beautiful," "broken," and "burdened." Someone should do some work on that.

ready, didn't you? Because you know your grandma. And because you know yourself.

We might have come from a church or family background that hammered home our individual brokenness, for example. Such a church would home in on the language of "sin" and "sinner" and "sinful" and "Sinny McSinnington" to talk about humanity and our deep need for Jesus and the grace that is ours through his death. You could be faithfully attending that church and praying daily for forgiveness . . . while you're also faithfully attending therapy with a wise counselor who is helping you see your own beauty as a first step to recognizing the beauty of the world around you. And at some point you could become aware that you've been carrying a heavy weight bound to your back by patriarchy, or homophobia, or racism. And there it all is, swirled together in the complex deliciousness of beautiful, broken, burdened you.

Dear reader, can I suggest that you take a minute at this point to think about yourself and where you came from; and what you were told about yourself and other human beings when you were very young; and which parts of what you were told you have held on to, and which parts you have let go? Just put the book down. Write "beautiful," "broken," and "burdened" on a piece of paper. Scribble some thoughts about your own sense of self, your experiences with other humans, who told you what about all that, the ways you have changed your mind or learned new insights with respect to those categories. Make your own categories if you don't like mine. Make it messy, because you are messy. Make it colorful, because you are colorful.

And when you are done, come back to this page, and hear me say again, in answer to the question "What does God want?" that what God wants . . .

. . . is you. All of you. Your whole beautiful, broken, burdened self.

And if God gets everything God wants, and we want to want more of what God wants, then all that's really being asked of us is that we show up, with our whole selves, and that we make spaces where other beautiful, broken, burdened humans can show up too.

That can be harder than it sounds, on a first reading. There are so many places where *part* of oneself is welcome, but not the *whole* self. We're taught to compartmentalize or fragment our personhood, bringing to each context only the segment of self that is acceptable or useful there.

Maybe you've learned that your job is not the place to express the hopes or heartaches of your personal life. Maybe your family can't appreciate your work frustrations or celebrations. Maybe you have secretly (or not so secretly) wished that coworkers would stay in the lane that is meant for such relationships, or that your beloveds would leave their work at work.

What I could not see until I was lucky enough to get oodles and oodles of queer people in my life is that the *church* has been complicit in asking people to be less than their whole self *when they are with the church*. I started understanding that I had always worshipped alongside LGBTQ+ people; I just hadn't known it because they hadn't been free to share that aspect of themselves in church. Sometimes that meant simply keeping quiet about their orientation; sometimes that meant hiding relationships, never celebrating or grieving the normal ups and downs of family life with the church. This was true in the conserving churches of my youth, where cis-straight was the only "right" way to be, but it was also true in the liberating churches of my adulthood, where "don't ask, don't tell" was the operative way of "dealing with" LGBTQ+ identity. A church elder in a mainline Protestant congregation once said to me, "I'm fine with them being here, but I don't ever want to hear about it."

When I finally had ears to hear it, I learned that LGBTQ+ Christians were reluctant experts on how to hide or ignore or suppress huge chunks of their very own hearts. The churches they were part of made them do it. * When they trusted me enough, they told me how heavenly they thought it might be to simply be the same person all the time, even and especially at church.

Does Your Church Want as Much of You as God Wants?

It made me think about all the ways the church colludes with society's requirement of intrapersonal fragmentation, and for all of us, not just queer Christians. When I was a child, for example, the clothing in my closet was clearly divided into two sets: a large set of "play clothes" (in the summertime) or "school clothes" (during the school year, natch), and a smaller set of "church clothes," kept apart from the rest. Changing outfits before attending any gathering of the church was a normal part of the Sunday morning, Sunday night, Wednesday night routine. I'm not opposed to wearing something special to a worship service, but I'm asking: what were we learning about the integrity, the wholeness, of the human person by doing that?

And isn't that the same impulse that has produced the litany that most of us are familiar with when we approach the door of the church just before worship starts? There's a person planted there to smile and say, "Hi, how're y'all?" while they hand you a printed bulletin. And the expected answer is, say it with me, and with a smile: "We're fine, just fine. How're y'all?" In some churches that's the first and last conversation you'll have with anyone, Sunday after Sunday—unless you wait patiently in the line at the back of the sanctuary when it's all over to shake the pastor's hand and say, "Nice sermon," to which she'll say, "Thanks, and it's so good to see you again." Sunday after Sunday, world without end, amen, amen.

---

* Sometimes they were also experts at hiding their Christian faith from queer friends who thought of churchgoing as a dangerous codependence with an abusive system. At Galileo Church we know not to tag anybody in photos we post on social media, in part because not everybody's "out" as a Christian. Go figure.

Interruptions to these litanies do happen; people sometimes feel safe in those transitional spaces to report the truth, that they are *not* fine, that they have need of prayer or whatever good mojo you've got that might help. But the person whose vulnerable transparency comes in too hot, too public, too often—you know the person I mean—is the exception that proves the rule, and is sometimes discussed as a problem in need of solving.

We have sought to make Galileo Church a place where the whole person that you are—beautiful, broken, and burdened—queer or not—is most welcome. No, that's not quite right; "we have sought" makes it sound much more deliberate and formal than it has been. What we've actually said is, it's a missional priority of our church to "do real relationship, no bullshit, ever." Because we think that's what God wants, and we want to want what God wants, even when sometimes a little less realness and a little more bullshit would be easier.

And while we're being honest, I should also say: we're most likely at Galileo Church to talk about ourselves and other people as beautiful and burdened. "Broken" is not, shall we say, top of mind for us right now. The spiritual refugees who gather at Galileo have had quite a lot of "broken" drilled into our spirits. Here in the Bible Belt, where everybody grew up Baptist or Church of Christ or some other flavor of fundagelical, we just . . . we already *know* we've made tons of mistakes and hurt tons of people, and we're well aware that we each have the capacity to do more of that anytime. For lots of us, it was our very identity that was pegged as deeply broken/sinful and in need of repair/forgiveness. The language of sin and forgiveness loses a lot of nuance (and kindness) when it's aimed at something so core to your being.

So we don't talk about (or sing about or pray about) the brokenness so much. I'm not saying "never"; we sing "Amazing Grace" once in a while, and we do pray the Lord's Prayer together in earnest each week, confessing our brokenness ("forgive us our sins")—and in the same breath reminding God that we're burdened ("as we forgive those who sin against us"). We've grown in our awareness that we participate in the burdening of some, exactly because, like everybody else on every rung of that ladder, we're broken. I think it's safe to say that Galileo Church folx are not any more or less self-interested, self-deceived, or self-destructive (i.e., sinful) than people in the Sinny McSinnington churches. Not exactly sure how we would test that theory.

But getting back to *you*, and how what God wants is all of you: what would it take for a church to be the first place you felt like you could be your whole beautiful, broken, burdened self? I wrote a memoir of Galileo Church's first five years* that tells stories about queer people experiencing the church as a safe space to come out, bring (or find) a date, show affection to their partner, dress in the clothes that make them feel most like themselves. And I wrote about what it feels like to me, a cis-het pastor who used to wrap up my pastor-self in a tidy package called "Reverend Katie," to now be part of a church where I'm expected to show up completely, not my "Reverend" persona but really me, beautiful, broken, and burdened just like everybody else.

Spoiler alert, in case you haven't read that memoir: it feels really, really, really good. It feels like God getting a little bit more of everything God wants. It feels like a little bitty bit of heaven on earth.**

---

* *We Were Spiritual Refugees: A Story to Help You Believe in Church* (2020). *Publishers Weekly* said it was "illuminating, animated, and unwieldy." Which I have taken as my personal vision statement.

** Stop right here for a singing break. Cue up Belinda Carlisle's "Heaven Is a Place on Earth" and belt it out. It's one of our favorite songs for worship. We probably sing it more often than "Amazing Grace," now that I think about it.

10

GOD WANTS YOU, BAPTIZED

You didn't understand it, of course you didn't. Nobody understands it when it first happens. Most people don't even really remember how it happened, or where or when or why. Whenever I ask people to tell me about their baptism, they get squirmy and confessional. It turns out that *lots* of baptized people are uncomfortable or even unhappy with the way their baptism went down. Maybe they know that Galileo Church dunks people completely under water, and they were "only" sprinkled. Maybe they realize that our church baptizes people who want it for themselves, and they were "only" a baby. Maybe now they're twenty-two, or thirty-two, or fifty-two, and they know so much more now than when they were "only" twelve, the ripe old "age of accountability" that's pretty typical for lots of baptisms where I'm from.

It's a hazard of doing theological rehabilitation. If our towers have fallen down, and we've cleared away the rubble and found the golden nuggets that belong in our very core, and we're patiently reconstructing Christian faith in the company of a brand-new community of belonging in Jesus's name, it feels like starting completely over. No wonder people wonder if they *should* start completely over, be born again *again*, to get it right this time.

"But listen," I counsel, "if we filled up this cattle trough* and

---

* Yes, our baptistery is really a cattle trough. Three hundred gallons, Rubber-

108

dunked you right now, with your head and heart filled to the brim with everything you've unlearned and relearned about God, the universe, and everything, you'd be right back here in five or ten or twenty years, saying you didn't know a damn thing *today*. God is always going to be showing us something new we couldn't have understood before, if we're doing this right. You don't need a new baptism. You just need to grow into the one you've already got."*

Contemplate Your Baptism

Growing into the baptism you've got challenges, for a lot of us, our previous understanding that baptism is simply a requirement for admission—into the church, into God's heart, into the afterlife geography called "heaven." Rather than thinking of baptism as a task on a list that can be accomplished and scribbled through (though I surely do love scribbling through tasks on lists), what if it became an *identity*, a way of naming our own being, that encompasses and changes and relativizes everything else about us?

When "I'm beautiful" is baptized, vanity dissolves and other-centered virtues like kindness and generosity bubble to the surface.

When "I'm broken" is baptized, shame floats away and mercy for self and others soaks in.

When "I'm burdened" is baptized, helplessness drowns, and courage and hope are raised up.

People who become co-conspirators with Galileo Church live into their commitment to the community in a number of ways that

---

maid heavy-duty plastic, encased in weathered fence wood so it looks like a hot tub at the front of our worship space in the Big Red Barn.

* I'm quick to confess that I'm a double-dunker myself, having been baptized at twelve only to decide at fifteen that I didn't understand what I was doing when I was twelve. My fifty-one-year-old self chuckles to think how much wiser I was (not) at fifteen than at twelve. I'm grateful to the wise souls who have kept me out of the do-over water in all the years since then.

we enumerate.* First on that list is "Contemplate your baptism, past or future." We want to make it clear that not having been baptized is not a barrier to belonging, and equally clear that having done the deed does not release us from its obligation. Indeed, *getting* baptized is simply the prerequisite for *being* baptized, if you catch my drift.

I've heard the story about Martin Luther and his baptism so many different ways. I've heard that he carved "I AM BAPTIZED" into his desk so he'd see it while he worked, or that he wrote it on the desk in chalk every day as he got started. I've heard it was on a plaque hung on the wall at the foot of his bed, so that it was the first thing he saw when he opened his eyes in the morning: "REMEMBER, YOU ARE BAPTIZED." The way I usually tell it is the way I heard it first: that every morning, when his mind awakened from sleep and he became aware of the new day, he whispered to himself, "Remember, Martin, you are baptized."

What we know for sure is that the sixteenth-century Protestant reformer told his congregation often to "remember their baptism" — not meaning a recollection of the event itself, since it's unlikely any of his parishioners could have remembered the sprinkling they received as infants. For Luther, baptism was an identity that made all the difference every day. "I'm beautiful," "I'm broken," and "I'm burdened" could all still be true, along with "I'm queer," "I'm white," "I'm Black," "I'm female," "I'm trans," "I'm autistic," "I'm any-variety-of-human-identity"; but all these identities would be *baptized* identities. And that would change everything.

For one thing, your baptized identity would mean that God has said yes to the person you are: beautiful, broken, and burdened. God has invited you into partnership, into the bending of the moral universe's arc toward love on a public scale. God wants *you*, all of

---

* The document that describes Galileo's co-conspiracy can be found on the church's website, galileochurch.org. Go to "This Is Us," then scroll down to "Join the Conspiracy."

you, engaged in that project alongside God. We contemplate God's yes in baptism at Galileo Church by remembering Jesus's own baptism, and claiming the blessing God spoke to him as our own.* Some Sundays we pour water over each other's hands (not an actual baptism but a memory of one) and say the words: "[Your Name Here], you are God's child, and you are so loved. God is so pleased with you."

You Said Yes

For another thing, your baptized identity would mean you have said yes to God getting everything God wants.** You've enlisted your whole being in wanting more of that—which likely also means saying no to the self-generated wants we all know quite well. Over a lifetime of growing into it, our baptism melts away pride and prejudice. And it transforms privilege and power so that they can be relinquished or leveraged for the sake of God's dream for the cosmos.

So when we take up justice causes at Galileo Church, we take them up as *baptized* people, believing that our baptisms call us to Christian witness in public places. Our church's local and state political culture is quite conserving, meaning that when we lobby our elected officials to do justice for LGBTQ+ people, we know before we start that we're unlikely to get what we hope for easily or quickly.

---

* "And just as he was coming up out of the water, he saw the heavens torn apart and the Spirit descending like a dove on him. And a voice came from heaven, 'You are my Son, the Beloved; with you I am well pleased'" (Mark 1:10-11).

** Yep, even if it happened when you were a baby. At some point, through a confirmation class or maybe just through your own human maturation, you adopted your own baptism—consented to it, if you will. (Unless, of course, you didn't. But then you wouldn't be reading this book, now, would you?) Anyway, it's kinda like the adolescent who yells at their parent, "I didn't *ask* to be born!" Well, neither did you ask to be born again, if someone else agreed to it on your behalf. But here you are, still baptized. Say yes if you haven't already, and get on with it!

But we do the work anyway, naming our commitment to want what God wants as our motivation. "Because we are Christian, we want justice for LGBTQ+ employees written into school district policy," we might say (and have said, so very many times). As baptized people with baptized identities, we hang all our baptized weight on the arc of the moral universe, hoping to bend it just a bit more toward God getting everything God wants.

I hope that sounds as impossibly *large* as it is—that by our baptisms we are each drafted onto God's team, invited and agreeing to collaborate with the God of the universe to get God everything God wants. Far from a once-and-done ritual, baptism marks the start of a lifelong quest to spend our lives (our time, our energy, our giftedness, our material resources, whatever we've got as real skin in the game) in service of GGEGW.

But I would stress that for most of us, the fulfillment of that agreement has mostly to do with the ordinary, daily living of our baptized lives. We're making a kajillion decisions every day, but we're making them *baptized*. That is, we're doing what we do in ways that are good for the world God loves, the world that God is even now at work to rehabilitate and re-create into God's dream of how the world should work. Our baptisms drench every decision every day.

We used to imagine that only people like me—ordained, and on the church's payroll—could speak of a calling, a *vocation*, in service of God's reign. But a fuller understanding of baptism as a kind of enrollment in God's ongoing project has meant reimagining all our work, all our living, as called and empowered and ordained and blessed by God, and potentially good for the world God loves.

So I'm writing this book, and I'm writing it *baptized*, thinking about how and whether it might be good for the world God loves, to launch these ideas beyond the walls of Galileo's Big Red Barn. (And remembering that actually *writing* instead of frittering away my writing leave by *worrying* about writing is better.) You are tending bar, and you're bartending *baptized*, thinking about how your kindness to lonely patrons and your firmness in never letting anybody drive home drunk is good for the world God loves.

Or you're raising kids, and you're parenting *baptized*, thinking about how the generous, kind adults you're cooking will be good for the world God loves. Or you're practicing law, and you're lawyering *baptized*, thinking about how the system you influence has the capacity to add to or deplete the store of justice in the world God loves. Or you're grading students' papers. Or you're coaching a team. Or you're serving people dinner. Or you're cleaning someone's office. You're doing what you do, and doing it *baptized*, so that the energy you expend makes a little more of what God wants, just a little, every day of the world, amen, amen.

This may or may not be the life you were born for. But it is absolutely the life you were born again for.

You are God's child. You are so loved. God is so pleased with you.

Jesus, the Humanest Human

#unpopularopinion: When it comes to our baptized lives, Christians should get more of our understanding from Jesus and less from Paul. I'm not saying Paul's own baptismal theology isn't terrific, brilliant, powerful. It's just that we've leaned heavily on his idea of baptism-into-Christ without giving enough attention to Christ's own baptized life and what it says about ours.

From Paul, we got our understanding of baptism as the washing away of sin, the putting to death of self, and the rising into new life "in Christ."* And while I believe, à la Paul, that my baptismal union with Christ is a metaphysical reality conferred by the sacrament,

---

* We also got a gorgeous prophetic vision of baptized identity in Galatians 3:28, as discussed in the "Catching On" chapter. I'm not dissing Paul, truly. Just asking if we can turn our attention elsewhere for a minute in case there's something we missed.

I also believe we're meant to learn from Jesus what it looks like to live this life, walk this earth, be in this world as one baptized into the reign-of-God project he was so obsessed with. If my life project is to want what God wants, and spend myself in service of that wanting, it helps to look to Jesus, because he went first and showed us how. The "pioneer and perfecter of our faith," he is somewhere called, * meaning he's been here, done this, and he can show us the way.

Jesus himself invited emulation. When he talked to his friends about his role among us, describing what he was doing here with his one wild and precious life, he usually called himself "the Son of Humanity," according to the Gospels. Well, he said "Son of *Anthropos*," which English translations are irritatingly consistent in rendering "Son of Man." But this is "man" in the collective sense of "human beings," and we have an English word for that that doesn't leave out half the population. It's high time we used it.

You can find Jesus talking about himself in this weird, third-person way in all the Gospels. Some of my faves:

And Jesus said to him, "Foxes have holes, and birds of the air have nests; but the Son of [Humanity] has nowhere to lay his head." (Matt. 8:20)

"So that you may know that the Son of [Humanity] has authority on earth to forgive sins"—he said to the paralytic—"I say to you, stand up, take your mat and go to your home." (Mark 2:10-11)

"The Son of [Humanity] has come eating and drinking, and you say, 'Look, a glutton and a drunkard, a friend of tax collectors and sinners!'" (Luke 7:34)

---

* JK. Not "somewhere," but Hebrews 12:2.

> So Jesus said to them, "Very truly, I tell you, unless you eat the
> flesh of the Son of [Humanity] and drink his blood, you have
> no life in you." (John 6:53)*

It's important to know that Jesus didn't make up that nickname.
He plucked it right out of the Hebrew Bible, where the mostly plural
"sons of humanity" means "generations of human beings" as distinct from heavenly beings, and distinct from God's own self. It just
means "ordinary people," and it's used a lot that way in the Bible
Jesus read.**

But then there's Daniel, a Hebrew Bible prophet who had a
sci-fi-style vision of the End of the World as We Know It—i.e., the
great remodeling of the universe to reflect God's dream. Daniel said
he saw a figure "like a human being," somebody *like us*, and this
somebody-like-us is so integral to God's remodeling project that
God puts that one in charge of the whole thing:

> As I watched in the night visions,
>   I saw *one like a human being*
>   coming with the clouds of heaven.
>   And he came to the Ancient One
>   and was presented before him.
> To him was given dominion
>   and glory and kingship,
>   that all peoples, nations, and languages
>   should serve him.
>   His dominion is an everlasting dominion
>   that shall not pass away,

---

* This last one—not actually one of my faves; actually kind of creepy. But still.
** The prophet Ezekiel was repeatedly addressed by God as "Son of Humanity"—
translated "Mortal" in the NRSV. An endearing nickname? A reminder of the
ontological gulf between God and Zeke? Both?

and his kingship is one
that shall never be destroyed. (Dan. 7:13–14,
emphasis added)

In Jesus's Bible, "one like a human being" from Daniel's vision was translated as "one like a son of humanity," and that's the identity Jesus took for himself, turning the phrase into a proper noun, the Son of Humanity: somebody like us, integral to God getting everything God wants.

"Son of Humanity" understood as "somebody like us" gives us a lot to work with. Jesus is a baby, then a kid who grows into adulthood. Jesus gets a stomachache from eating bad fish.* Jesus has to learn what he doesn't yet know, and maybe makes mistakes along the way because that's how humans learn. Jesus gets mad. Jesus feels sad. Jesus likes parties. Jesus is rude to his mom.** Jesus has friends who are good to him, friends who are shitty to him, and some actual enemies. And, like all humans, Jesus has a lifespan. At the end of it, he dies.***

Just like us.

But the "just like us" traffic goes both directions. If the Word-of-God-Become-Flesh is "just like us" in all our human frailty, it's also true that the Son of Humanity is a kind of living demonstration of what human being (not *a* human being, but human *being*) *could* look like when done really, really well. You want to know how to

---

* That's not actually in the Bible. It's just from my imagination, that Jesus, if he is "somebody like us," occasionally suffered gastrointestinal distress.

** For real, Mark 3:31–35, if you are a mom, can't be read any other way. I half expect Mary to yell back, "Twenty-eight hours! Twenty-eight hours I labored to bring you into this world . . ."

*** Indeed, when we're talking about "why Jesus had to die," hunting around for theories of atonement that don't make God look like a giant asshole who demands Big Suffering in payment for the brokenness we inherited and can't escape on our own, we tend to overlook this fact about mortality. If Jesus is just like us, he has to die. Because *we* die. The Son of Humanity can't *not* die. There was never going to be any other ending to that story.

be human? Look at Jesus, the humanest human, the archetypal human, not just *a* son of humanity, but *the* Son of Humanity. He shows us how to human at the highest level.* He's just like us, so that we can be just like him.

And while we might wish for more stories of Jesus as a kid and a teenager and a young man just getting the hang of #adulting, it's instructive that we know pretty much nothing about him until his baptism. We're not even really sure how he got there, to the muddy banks of the Jordan River; and we aren't invited to spend any time with him until he and God say yes to each other in that river and his baptized life begins in earnest. The only Jesus we know, the Humanest Human, is *baptized* Jesus, his own identity drenched in cooperative concordance with God's dream for the world God loves.

And—here's where this is all going—our own baptized selves, our own identities soaked in Jesus's baptized identity ("in Christ," like Paul says!), now have something to shoot for in terms of our own humanity. We know how to be human because we know how Jesus, the very Son of Humanity, the very Humanest Human, was human.

---

* I grew up around FFA and 4-H, not in either one myself but a jealous spectator when other Texas school kids got to skip class for weeklong stock shows. When my cousin took up the discipline of evaluating chickens, which involved sticking his fingers up their bums to gauge their egg-laying capacity, I stopped being jealous. The idea of judging farm stock (i.e., animals) is to learn what characteristics make a particular animal the ideal specimen of their particular breed. Picture Jesus as an entry in a stock show for humans. He's the prize-winning human, a damn fine specimen, the humanest human there ever was.

II

HUMANING LIKE THE HUMANEST HUMAN

Thinking about it this way—How can we model our humanity after the Humanest Human at his most human?—has yielded answers at Galileo Church that shape our lives, and our life together, in ways we didn't expect. For your consideration: Four ways to human the way Jesus humaned. (I know it's grammatically messy. Just go with it and see what happens.)

There's no shame in a swing and a miss.

Remember that time the Son of Humanity needed a vacation, and he went to an out-of-the-way seaside resort where he thought he wouldn't be recognized?* I like to imagine him relaxing on the beach holding a bright pink drink with a paper umbrella in it. But word got out— paparazzi everywhere, tweeting his location?—and a Gentile woman came on over and knelt in the sand to ask a favor: healing for her little daughter. Jesus, still running his choo-choo on the one-ethnicity track, said, "Nah." It was rude, and we all know it; or maybe we should celebrate that he had well-defined *boundaries* for his vocation and his vacation? But when the woman pressed him with the kind of good argument mama bears are known for making, he said, "Huh." And he reconsidered, and the woman's little daughter was fine.

---

* You can refresh your memory in Mark 7:24–30.

One thing I know for sure: if you and I spend enough time together, I'm eventually going to make a mistake that hurts your feelings, or pisses you off, or keeps you from getting something you really need. Or maybe you'll go first, and I'll be the dog begging scraps under your table. Either way, the Son of Humanity's modeling of human *being* tells me that this is OK. Some mistakes aren't born of meanness or malice; they're truly our best swing, and *whiff!* The ball goes right by. This is how we learn important things about being in real relationship with each other. It's the same way Jesus learned, and if it's good enough for him . . .

This is also an indispensable piece of our contemplation of our baptisms. Because if I'm onto something with that thing about baptism as something we grow into over time, there are guaranteed to be mistakes along the way. If the Son of Humanity didn't already understand, the very moment he emerged from the baptismal waters, every single thing God had in mind for the good of the world God still loves and his own place in it, how could we? Life is for learning. The baptized life is for learning more and more and more about what God wants, and how we can want more of that too. May we never figure it all out!

Niceness is not a Christian virtue.

Remember that time the Son of Humanity said something really harsh about the VRPs (Very Religious Persons), right out loud, in front of other people, and they got their feelings hurt? Well, actually, there were lots of times like that, but the one I'm thinking of comes right before his beach vacay to Tyre. Maybe this is the confrontation that made him think he needed a beach vacay.

The way Matthew tells it,* some VRPs started hassling him about his disciples' failure to keep up a ritual practice for religious

---

*   Matt. 15:1–20.

purity.* When Jesus snapped back with a far weightier condemnation—one I suspect he was keeping in his back pocket for a moment just like this—his disciples got flustered and came at him with an age-old pretense for complaining to your pastor: "This is not necessarily what *we* think, but we think you should know, some people are saying . . ." In this case, "some people were saying" that Jesus's frank and public assessment of the VRPs' hypocrisy was "offensive." And Jesus was like, "You think *that's* offensive? Boys, I haven't even gotten wound up yet." Next thing you know, he's talking about how wholesome, natural, and good it is to poop out your food, and how unwholesome, unnatural, and *not* good it is to poop out the evil intentions of your heart. I'm serious. That's what he said.

So there was that one time. And there were a bunch of other times that Jesus kinda came unhinged at the VRPs (see Matt. 23:13–38, for example), at his disciples (Mark 9:19, for example), at the temple capitalists (turning over tables! spilling the money boxes! chasing out animals and humans alike!), at an innocent fig tree (Mark 11:13–14, 20–22! It wasn't even the season for figs!)—it all adds up to the Son of Humanity being altogether unconcerned with niceness. Or, at least this: he did not spend an ounce of his baptized energy trying to be the most well behaved and well liked among other humans.

I wouldn't say this is license to be cranky for no good reason. But I have learned to say no to the false teaching that Christian discipleship means being polite so as never to cause offense. Sometimes my own baptized humanity takes after the baptized Son of Humanity in the "Did you know they were offended by what you said?" vein, especially where injustice has needed naming. It's not *nice* to talk that way, but sometimes it's *Christian*.

---

* Handwashing before a meal, actually, which Jesus's friends didn't do, which kinda grosses me out since I'm writing during a global pandemic; but neither Jesus nor his friends nor his enemies knew about microorganisms. The kind of handwashing they were talking about was more like hygiene theater—for the soul.

You are a grown-ass adult, imbued with the Spirit of the living Christ.

This goes back to part 3, about God giving power away, and about the partnership we're called into so we can contribute to God getting more of what God wants. If it's baptism that seals the deal—which is available to every human, not a specialty sacrament meant for a few (like ordination to ministry, e.g.)—then it's important that we recognize and honor that capacity in ourselves and in each other.

Christian community hasn't always treated people this way. Indeed, churches can be downright condescending, building doctrine-discerning and decision-making infrastructure that is inaccessible to most of the people in the church. In some forms of church, that looks like only certain people, designated for the church's best and holiest work, being allowed to serve communion or handle the Bible or lead liturgy or convene a prayer group. In others, leadership structures are sealed off from the young, the single, or pretty much anybody who doesn't fit a kind of corporate respectability mold.

But mostly, in the small churches I've served, it just looks like people being very clear about where the power lies, even while the processes by which power is exercised are kept mostly obscure to most of the church.

All of which leads me to ask, what if the church took its members' baptisms seriously? What if the church actually *believed* that believers are imbued with the Spirit of the living Christ, like Peter believed it about Cornelius, like Paul believed it about oodles and oodles of people like me? What if we believed the dove from heaven descends on every believer, just like it did Jesus, when they come up out of the water? What if each person in the church were taught that, at their baptism, they start becoming more and more capable of and responsible for *knowing what to do*? What if it were *not* the responsibility of clergy to tell people how to behave, or to articulate every prayer, or to be the Decider of the direction for what comes next in the life of the church—i.e., to infantilize the church in order to preserve a kind of parental authority?

At Galileo Church, I'm never sad to be asked my opinion about what someone should do with their life, or how they should respond to a particular heartache or nurture a particular hope. I'm glad to be invited into people's discernment about family life, parenting life, work life, spiritual life, political life, ethical life, economic life, health-and-wellness life. But honestly, upon being asked for my help, I'm very likely to hit it back over the net: "Hmm. What do *you* think?" Because most every time, the person sitting right in front of me is a grown-ass adult imbued with the Spirit of the living Christ.

That's basically what Jesus said, when it was time for him to take a hike and leave his life's work in the hands of some of the world's most mediocre people. Depending on whose memory you trust, he either (a) apparated into their hidey-hole and silently exhaled his very own Spirit into their faces (the John 20 version),* or (b) he asked them to give him a couple days to get home and get his stuff set up, then poured out the Spirit from the heavens with a laser-light show and a heavy metal, bass-thumping soundtrack.**

Either way, the point is the same: the Holy Spirit who previously got credit for burning bushes and water wells in the desert is now *in people*, using our hands and feet and mouths and minds and energy to get God more of what God wants.*** If we can't see that in ourselves,

---

* Which, in a literary allusion typical for John, is a recapitulation of Genesis 2:7, where God blows the breath (Spirit!) of life into the first human.

** Luke 24:49, then Acts 2.

*** "Christ has no body now but yours. No hands, no feet on earth but yours. Yours are the eyes through which he looks with compassion on this world. Yours are the feet with which he walks to do good. Yours are the hands through which he blesses all the world. Yours are the hands, yours are the feet, yours are the eyes, you are his body. Christ has no body now on earth but yours."—Teresa of Avila, sixteenth century.

and in each other, we end up with a dormant faith that politely and passively waits for God to get everything God wants, terrified to take risks, reading our Bibles for comforting confirmation of what we've already been told it says. But if we are grown-ass adults imbued with the Spirit of the living Christ—holy cow. We've got stuff to *do*.

That means the church should stay out of the way of Christians' compulsion to cooperate with the Spirit. At Galileo Church, if someone is moved with compassion for hungry kids, say, it's not necessary for them to petition the church to start a Feed the Kids program. They can find out where that work is happening already and join in with joy; they can harness the resources of the church (space, money, chairs, excellent Wi-Fi) to help make it happen. Like Jesus sending out apostles to do reign-of-God things wherever they light,* the church that trusts the baptisms of its people deploys them in full confidence that they know how to get a little bit more of what God wants wherever they go.

Don't read your Bible alone.

This is a really hard one. Lots of times when spiritual refugees stagger through Galileo Church's door and start feeling themselves come back to life, spiritually speaking, they want to rededicate themselves to the project of being Christian. One of the ways they've been told in the past they can prove their reengaged faithfulness is by a renewed commitment to private spiritual disciplines, especially Bible reading. When they announce to me proudly that they're going to read through the Bible in a year, or rejigger their morning routine to include daily devotions, I wince (mostly) on the inside.

Because the Bible is not for sissies, y'all. It's uneven and unkind and uninspiring in places. It's unapologetically misogynistic and

---

* Mark 6:7-13.

pro-enslavement and heteronormative and genocidal and racist and violent. You can argue with me if you want, but I'll win, because I've read it *all*, and lots of it is just really, really hard to squeeze any little drop of gospel out of. The Bible can be dangerous to the reader, especially readers who have been beaten up by the Bible in churches past and are trying their hardest to believe us when we say that God's *love* is the engine that powers the universe. We get that from the Bible, yes; but sometimes we are gleaning that love from the narrow edges of wide fields full of other, not-so-loving stuff.

I'm not saying *don't* read the Bible; I'm just saying, read it like the Son of Humanity did. Jesus read scripture in the synagogues, from shared scrolls, in the company of his religious kin. He inherited a traditional practice of reading aloud and then discussing together what the text had meant in times past and could mean now. He didn't own a Bible of his own; nobody did.* It was his habit to spend Sabbath days in Bible study *with the community of believers.*

If you have a Bible app that lets you search for words, do a quick one for "synagogue" in the Gospels, and count how many times Jesus shows up in one. Or take Luke's word for it: "When he came to Nazareth, where he had been brought up, he went to the synagogue on the sabbath day, *as was his custom*" (Luke 4:16a, emphasis added).

My point is: reading the Bible in the discerning company of trusted religious kin can be maximally helpful in learning to want more of what God wants; reading the Bible alone, not so much. I may be pressing this a bit too far, but the Son of Humanity pressed for and participated in *community* for his own spiritual flourishing. We Western, white, individualistic-to-a-fault folx are the ones who turned Christianity into an autonomous exercise in personal piety.

---

* Indeed, nobody *would* for another millennium and a half, until Herr Gutenberg's printing press stamped out pages cheaply enough for wide distribution. Then all that had to happen was for literacy rates to catch up to the technology.

The Son of Humanity read his Bible with his friends, and we should definitely consider doing more of the same.

Yep, I'm aware of Jesus's habit of seeking solitude for prayer, and his instructions for us to seek some alone time in the prayer closet ourselves. But the American Christian pendulum has swung ve-e-e-ery far in the direction of pious individualism, don't you think? We could really use a corrective in this regard, looking to our churches as communities of cooperative exploration, learning, and discernment. If we talked exclusively about the "y'all" of scripture (see the next chapter) for the next hundred years, we might still not have sorted out the entanglement of American individualism with Christian doctrine and practice.

You get people. A church, even.

Grown-ass adults that we each are, imbued with the Spirit of the living Christ as we each are, we still should not imagine ourselves on our own in the project of becoming fully human in the way of Jesus, fully baptized, fully partnered up with God for God's achievement of God's dream. Indeed, Jesus seemed to understand from the very start that he needed some people to support his reign-of-God project, his own baptized, wanting-to-want-what-God-wants life. And if he did, then there's no way we *don't*, which gets us to our next point, in part 5:

God wants you (and everybody else) to have people.

Yeah, like a church.

Or even, yeah, a church.

PART FIVE

WE WANT TO WANT WHAT GOD WANTS

12

SAYING YES TO EACH OTHER

God says yes to you; you say yes to God; and here's one more
thing, for now, that the contemplation of your baptism helps
you remember:

In baptism, we say yes to each other.

God doesn't need the church, but God knows we do.

It may feel singular in the moment, like you're the only one who's
dripping wet and hoping the clothes you chose for the occasion of
your public drowning are appropriately obscuring all your nooks
and crannies. But when you're baptized, you get people. You get a
community of belonging in Jesus's name. You get a *church*, whether
you want one or not. *

It goes back to that thing Jesus-in-a-hamster-ball was always
doing: he was always breaking the hold of isolation by reconnecting
people with their people. Not just "take up your mat and walk" for
the mobility-impaired guy in Mark 2:1–12, but also "Go to your
home." Not just "Your faith has made you well" to the lepers of
Luke 17, but also "Go and show yourselves to the priests" (so they
could be pronounced religiously clean and readmitted to the com-

---

*   JK—of course you want one. I mean, if church were being what it's supposed
to be, you absolutely would.

pany of the synagogue). Not just a dead man raised to life in Luke 7, but Jesus "gave him to his mother."*

And it goes back to Paul's prophecy in Galatians 3:27–29 that when we "clothe ourselves with Christ" in baptism, when we "belong to Christ" in baptism, our various identities are subsumed in our baptism so that we are, all of us, "one in Christ Jesus." All of us, one in Christ—that is, all together in our *in-Christ-ness*.

I was surprised to learn that a particular person at Galileo Church had not been baptized. She had grown up in a church where the pressure to get dunked would have been intense in adolescence; she came from a devout family; her own faith was strong and getting stronger. *Why, then, had she not done it already?* I wondered. So I asked. And she said, without a second of hesitation, "Up to now, I've never been part of a church I wanted to belong to completely. I just couldn't say yes to a church that couldn't say yes to all of me." We baptized her a few Sundays later, and she got a church, and the church got all of her, and we are both the better for it.

It didn't happen all at once, though. Over the next couple of years, that young woman became more and more completely who she had always been, who God made her to be. Identified male at birth, her baptized self gradually owned up to the gender-queerness that had been true of herself all along. At church, she could wear what she wanted. At church, we used the pronouns she told us. At church, over time, she became more integrated, more emotion-

---

* This is one component of the case I make when I encounter the specious argument from some Christians that queer *orientation* is OK but queer *life* (i.e., sex, partnership, marriage, family) is not, meaning that LGBTQ+ persons can be welcome in the church so long as they maintain a lifelong commitment to celibacy. To that I say, "Bull hockey." When did Jesus ever choose to leave someone alone, bereft of relationship and family and community and love, and call it a day? Didn't he return people to their lost loves over and over and over again? The church that is the body of Christ, carrying on the ministry of Jesus, will never require some people to remain alone forever.

ally present, more *there*, and *more baptized* than she had been before. And the loneliness, the intense in-her-own-headness that she thought she had learned to live with, floated away in the baptismal waters, thanks be to God.

It would be hard to overstate what baptism into the people of God could mean to spiritual refugees, people who've learned that the church doesn't want or understand or love all of who they are. Most of the spiritual refugees I've ever met have lived with an isolating sadness for a long time, alone in their thoughts, alone in their wondering if even God wishes they were a little bit, or a whole lot, *less* than they are. When we are baptized into the company of believers, into the oneness Paul prophetically envisioned for the baptized people of God, into Jesus's reign-of-God cloud where lonely people get their people back, we are promising each other that we'll stick together. We're confirming that we're well aware of the beauty, the brokenness, and the burdens we're all bringing into the mix.

We're saying yes to all of that, and no to the impossible sine qua non of having a "personal relationship with Jesus Christ."* Don't freak out! I'm not saying that the God of the universe doesn't number the hairs on your head or know your true name or get your pronouns right every single time. I believe God does, absolutely, know the sequence of your DNA and God did, absolutely, know before you did that you were gay, or straight, or a 3 on the Enneagram, or whatever.

But I am saying that you and I are not equipped to carry our half of a relationship with the Deity of the universe, or the Word-of-God-Enfleshed, all by our lonesome. God is *a lot*. God is too much for any one of us, which is why we need each other. We want to want what God wants, but the weight of wanting that can crush a single human being. Together, we are so much stronger, and when

---

*   Yep, I went there.

one of us tuckers out temporarily, the rest of us can keep it going.*

It's a thing we say at Galileo Church sometimes: "Keep the faith, and if you can't today, I'll keep it for you for a while." It honors the reality that on any given day, some of us are atheists, or at least considering it. On those days when it's me, I'm an atheist in the company of the faith-full, and they are holding on, keeping the faith, for my sake. Thanks be to God.

If that feels problematic to you, because you're sure that belief is a minimum basic requirement for any member of a Christian church, consider this: "faith" is listed in the Bible as one possible gift of the Spirit. You could spin the wheel of Spirit-gifts and get prophecy, or healing, or tongues speaking, or some other stuff, or *faith* (1 Cor. 12:9). Doesn't that mean not everybody gets that one, just like not everybody gets tongues speaking? And if it does mean that, doesn't *that* mean faith doesn't come easy to every Christian? Doesn't that mean the church is supposed to make room for people who *don't* have it, or have to work really hard for it, or can't keep it going all the time? Many gifts, one body, right?** Our individual gifts combine for the good of the whole collaborative project of God getting everything God wants. One gift we desperately need among us is faith.

---

* I went to college the first time on a scholarship from the US Air Force's ROTC, which meant I had to go to boot camp (or the Air Force's version of it) after my sophomore year. Y'all, I am not what any branch of the military would call a physical specimen. When we would get in formation for morning runs, five across and six deep, my fellow cadets would shuffle me into the deep middle of the pack. I found I could run for miles with my buddies before and behind me. When I tired out (which they could discern because I think I whimpered like a little child), one of them would reach out and touch the small of my back with a single finger. No pressure; just a touch. Miraculously, I never failed to reach the end of the day's run.

** First Corinthians 12 is one of the "many gifts, one body" chapters about church life, along with Romans 12 and Ephesians 4.

I'm also saying that you and I are not equipped, all by ourselves, to confront the heavy disappointment of a world that is not yet what God wants. We're not made to singularly shoulder the burdens of other people's brokenness, or even our own. It's crushing sometimes, the sheer tonnage of grief and fear and rage in our hearts. Church doesn't make all your troubles go away, but when we're doing it right, we help each other carry the heaviest parts.

One time I got invited to a gathering of "community innovators," a bunch of creatives mostly half my age who are all thinking about how people still want to gather for holistic, spiritual nourishment even as traditional institutions, like the church, fade away.* Cross-Fit, the physical exercise franchise, was named as one of the new communities where people find their people and form families of choice, so that the gym becomes a kind of church.** There was a Presbyterian minister there who had given up his literal church gig to open a CrossFit gym, where in addition to regular workout sessions, he ran "worship workouts" a couple times every weekend. I got to try it out in the Harvard Divinity School chapel.

The thing I knew about CrossFit workouts is that they're physically grueling. The thing I didn't know about CrossFit workouts is that they're designed to be done in intentional partnership with other exercisers. So for my worship workout, I was assigned a very fit partner for whom I quickly became very grateful. Because every time we were assigned a certain number of burpees, or push-ups,

---

* The gathering was an early project of Harvard Divinity School's Ministry Innovation Fellows Casper ter Kuile and Angie Thurston, who have subsequently collaborated with Sue Phillips to build Sacred Design Lab, a firm that explores and contributes to the changing landscape of community and spiritual life. You can read their findings in "How We Gather" and other compilations at https:// sacred.design, under "Insights."

** Gay men could have told us that a long time ago, tbh.

or other tortures, our instructions were to complete that number *together*. Twenty burpees? If I could do three, Tyler promised, he could do seventeen. Forty push-ups—if I could do five now and five at the end, Tyler could do thirty in between. While we grunted and sweat and held each other's feet for sit-ups, the Presbyterian pastor prayed and read scripture and preached a little, in between instructing our next moves; but I don't think that's what made it feel like church to me. It felt like church because Tyler and I, we hit our goal, every time. Together.

Many gifts. One body.

Sign My Petition: "Y'all" in the Bible

I remain deeply disappointed that standard English doesn't have a plural, second-person pronoun for use in translating Paul's epistles to the early church. "Youse" or "you guys" or, my favorite (as a Texan), "y'all" would go a long way toward recovering the overwhelming majority of Paul's exhortations as instructions for the church as a whole, rather than individual Christians. The early (Eastern, Semitic, dark-skinned, community-oriented) church just didn't think very much about faith as a singular "you" project.

Using "y'all" in translating Paul would help rescue Christianity from the impossibly Western, white, individualistic corner that fundagelicals have painted us into, where sin is a problem each one of us has to solve and salvation is a prize each one of us has to win. What if, instead of each of us taking full responsibility for a raft of mostly inconsequential little-s sins we can tally each day and hope to erase by our fervent, individual prayers for forgiveness—what if, instead, we could acknowledge that we're soaking, all together, in capital-S Sin, in the capital-B Brokenness of the broken world that weighs us down, burdening us with heavy burdens we can't bear up under? For example:

What if, instead of insisting, "I'm not racist!" because *I* haven't *myself* lately said or done anything overtly nasty to assert white supremacy, I could instead own up to my inherited and semiconscious participation in a collective legacy of white supremacy and systemic racism, and admit the accrual of white privilege I didn't ask for but nonetheless enjoy? What if it were less about me and more about us, thus allowing me to see and speak the truth about the lingering toxicity of racism that poisons our country, our churches, our neighborhoods, and our very own hearts, and for which I have as much responsibility as any white person living? It might not feel like *mine*, but it is *ours* in this collective way of imagining ourselves as "one in Christ Jesus."

And what if, instead of imagining myself someday standing alone before God, singularly accountable for all my individual steps and missteps, I imagined myself in the eschatologically gathered throng of God's children, my salvation bound up in the cosmic redemption of all things? What if, I'm asking, *salvation itself is communal*, so that my salvation is bound up with yours, and yours with mine? Like this:

In him *y'all* also, when *y'all* had heard the word of truth, the gospel of *y'all's* salvation, and *y'all* had believed in him, *y'all* were marked with the seal of the promised Holy Spirit; this is the pledge of our inheritance toward redemption as God's own people, to the praise of [God's] glory. (Eph. 1:13–14, with Texan modifications by me)

Or this:

But *y'all* are a chosen race, a royal priesthood, a holy nation, God's own people, in order that *y'all* may proclaim the mighty acts of [God] who called *y'all* out of darkness into [God's] marvelous light.

135

> Once *y'all* were not a people,
>   but now *y'all* are God's people;
> once *y'all* had not received mercy,
>   but now *y'all* have received mercy. (1 Pet. 2:9–10,
>   with "y'alls" added by me, yeehaw)

It's only by imagining ourselves this way, all together, as God's big, saved, marked-with-the-seal-of-the-Holy-Spirit *people* (not *persons*), that we become the literal fulfillment of Jesus's literal promise to each of his followers. Remember that time his disciples got homesick, nostalgic for all they had left behind for the sake of joining up with that God-getting-everything-God-wants project of his?

> Peter began to say to him, "Look, we have left everything and followed you." Jesus said, "Truly I tell you, there is no one who has left house or brothers or sisters or mother or father or children or fields, for my sake and for the sake of the good news, who will not receive a hundredfold now in this age—houses, brothers and sisters, mothers and children, and fields, with persecutions—and in the age to come eternal life." (Mark 10:28–30)

As I've written elsewhere,* I have usually read those words of Jesus's with my heart in my throat. He's writing a check that the church might not be able to cash, you know? I mean, even if we use all the familial language in the church, calling each other "brother" or "sister" or "sibling," are we really ready to *be* family to each other?

---

* See especially *Family of Origin, Family of Choice* (Eerdmans, 2021), for which my coauthor, Susan Chiasson, interviewed LGBTQ+ folx about their relationships with the families they were born into after they came out on the queer rainbow. In every case, our queerly, dearly beloveds described how very necessary it was to have an alternate family, a family of choice, when their family of origin could not accept their full human identity.

Are we ready to be *home* for each other, resting and growing and flourishing safely in the shelter of each other?*

> 'Home is the place where, when you have to go there,
> They have to take you in.'
>   'I should have called it
> Something you somehow haven't to deserve.'**

Obviously, sometimes the church is 100 percent *not* ready for that. And if I'm going to argue that part of the "everything" God wants for you (and everybody else) is to have people, I'm going to have to tell the truth about that. Next chapter.

---

* See Mary Pipher's 1996 book *The Shelter of Each Other*, which argues convincingly that "extended families can weather things that would bring a nuclear family down." I think she's right, in some cases; my spouse and I asked my parents-in-law to come make their home with us after we read this book. But what about those cases where extended family has rejected one of their own? Then, Jesus says, the church becomes "the shelter of each other," and if that title hadn't already been taken, I'd have used it. Though if Pipher hadn't already thought of it, I probably wouldn't have either.

** "The Death of the Hired Man," Robert Frost. Have you read the whole thing? Lately? I had not. But then I did. Whoa. There's a whole argument in there, about whether the ne'er-do-well (prodigal?) who has returned seeking mercy after leaving his employers in the lurch ought to, instead, go to his brother's house to seek charity. The former employers speculate about how thoroughly his family of origin must despise him. Who will be family to the man who has none? Who are his people? Where is his home?

13

THE CHURCH HAS TO DO BETTER

I've mentioned atheists and atheism several times in these pages, maybe more than one would expect in a book about theology, or what we (try to) believe about God. But atheists and atheism get a chunk of my mindshare in my service to Galileo Church. It's probably because the spiritual refugees who wash up on our shore half-drowned and gasping for air, once they feel able to speak, often use their first words to tell me, "I don't believe any of this stuff* anymore." To which I have learned to say, "Thank you for telling me that. I believe you. I love you. Tell me more."**

The "tell me more" part is especially important because, just like we don't all mean the same thing when we make the word "G-o-d" with our mouths, everybody claiming atheism doesn't *dis*believe the same thing. Sometimes my work as a theologian-in-residence is to help people sort out what it is they *don't* believe in. And not

---

* Usually they don't say "stuff."

** I learned that from a terrific podcast I've listened to several times now, first on my own and then as material for small group discussions with church folx. It's called *Blue Babies Pink*, and it's the serialized memoir of B. T. Harman, a devout Christian from a conserving background, coming out as gay. Brett remembers the first time he articulated his sexual orientation to a trusted friend, and the friend responded, in short, "Thank you. I believe you. I love you. Tell me more." What an amazing formula for listening and learning in the name of love. Somebody embroider that on a pillow and I will buy it.

to put too fine a point on it, but what a lot of novice atheists don't believe in is not God but the gosh-dang *people* of God. In which case, my contribution to their spiritual flourishing is to help them untangle what they might believe about God from what they don't/ can't/won't believe about the church.

Atheists: Maybe It's the Church You Don't Believe In

One woman told me how, having not been raised in a religious family, she was afraid to go to church with her girlfriend. But her girlfriend derived so much pleasure from her faith, and all their friends from the church were lovely people, so the woman decided to go. And guess what? She loved it. She loved the sense of belonging she felt. She loved the sense of purpose it gave her, like her life meant something, or could mean something. She joined the newcomers' class. She asked to be baptized. She was all in, and the church's arms were wide open to her.

The hour before her scheduled baptism, she went to meet with church leaders, assuming they asked this of every new convert. She was ushered into a small room where men she did not know stood over her and told her that her baptism and subsequent church membership were contingent on her breaking up with her girlfriend. "We know you are gay, but if you want to be a Christian, you can't *be* gay," they said. "You can't *live the gay lifestyle*." She had no idea this was the church's position. She could not discern in that moment whether her girlfriend and all her friends from church knew. She fled, unbaptized, and reclaimed the unbelief that at least had never lied to her.

"And that's why I'm an atheist," she says to me.

And I say, "Yes. I'm so sorry. That's on us."

I've seen it countless times: the church, in its dogmatic insistence on conformity, in its perpetual confusion of itself with God, sets itself down squarely between people and God, not as a mediator or midwife but as a barrier to God's heart. The church can make Christian belief impossible. *

It accounts for at least some (most? all?) of the meteoric rise in "none" as a description of North Americans' religious affiliation. Fully 40 percent of American millennials identify with no religious institution or tradition, according to the Pew Research Center, ** and a whole bunch of those "nones" can be described accurately as "dones," meaning they were raised in church but don't want it anymore. We churchy people, including and especially the church's pastors, might like to imagine that this surge of unbelonging is a symptom of widespread societal malaise, particularly the degradation of Christian habitus by a corrosive culture of performance of "self" in the nihilistic theater of social media. I've thought a lot about it—I mean, I wrote that last sentence, didn't I?—and I think that it's partly true.

But when the church is functioning at its best—when it's drawing in spiritual refugees who hunger and thirst for justice (GGEGW) instead of turning them away for their lack of compliance with our normative niceness and exclusionary ethics—when the church is *being church*, it is a refuge from culture's corrosive, nihilistic hopelessness and hedonism and from the utilitarian fragmentation of the human family ruled by heartless empire. That's how it all started, remember? The defiant little church, under the boot of empire?

Spiritual but Not Religious

That's why a whole bunch of the "nones" and "dones" in Pew's research also identify as "spiritual"—not religious, no, not participat-

---

* This point is made poignantly in Rob Bell's *Love Wins: A Book About Heaven, Hell, and the Fate of Every Person Who Ever Lived* (2011). Sometimes people's failure to become or remain Christian is the fault of churches who are so bad at it. Bad at being Christian, I mean.

** Do I really have to footnote that claim? Aren't you swimming in that data already? Aren't you *living* it?

ing in the collective expression of faith on offer in religious institutions, rituals, traditions, and habits, but *spiritual*, tapping into the idea that the world as we know it is not all there is, and that humans have the capacity to see/hear/engage beyond or beneath material reality, for the sake of their own flourishing at the tippy-top of Maslow's hierarchy of needs.

"SBNR," or "spiritual but not religious," untethers one's individual spirituality from the religious collective of the church (or synagogue or mosque). That would have been unthinkable to our forebears in faith, even fifty years ago; a fulsome (Christian) spirituality outside church membership and participation didn't seem possible.* But maybe in this widespread season of institutional deconstruction and decline it's helpful to untangle the two and see what they have to say to each other.

SBNR, in my experience, makes ample room for people who want God to be true, to exist, but don't trust the people of God to make God's existence known. It rewards people's curious searching for surprising signs of grace or providence. It empowers the searcher's sense that, beyond the habits of religious participation, the Divine waits to connect meaningfully with each member of the human family.

But SBNR also leaves people mostly alone to answer life's hardest questions and weather life's roughest seasons. It deprives them of the comfort and companionship of "the shelter of each other." The satisfaction it yields is as uneven as my seasonal moods, dependent as it is on my initiative, my perseverance, my commitment.

"So what if," I ask eventually, after a lot of listening to my atheist friend who fled the baptism based on trickery, "what if it's not God

---

* It also seemed, to some in generations past, unnecessary. A giant in the academic field of practical theology, upon learning of Pew's early findings concerning SBNR, was heard to grumble, "I'm religious but not spiritual." He meant, I think, that going along with the church's prescribed program for Christian practice and faith was good enough for him, and why shouldn't it be for his kids and grandkids? To which I say, with all the love in my heart, "OK, boomer."

you don't believe in? What if what they showed you there was not-God, and you were right to flee it, smart and strong enough to get the hell outta there? What if you know enough about God and the world God still loves to know something about what God wants, if there is a God, and you still want that? What if what you need is people you can test until you trust them, so that if you do, when you do, you'll have plenty of room to consider again whether God is real? And, you know, some companions for the journey, which is likely to be a hella hard one, and exhausting if you don't have some help?"

"You mean church," she says flatly. She is clearly unimpressed.

"Yeah," I say sheepishly. "It's my hammer, so your problem must be a nail. If I'm wrong, please forgive. But you'll know soon enough, if you hang around. You already know we won't be perfect. But we're doing the best we can to be good for the world, and you're most welcome to stay and do it with us, whatever you decide about God. Because I already know you love this world, just like God does. I also think I should tell you, the God I believe in is not waiting for you to figure this out before God can love you. Or before I can."

She stays. As of this writing, she's still here. I have to think that this is God, getting a little bit more of what God wants. Thanks be to the God she may or may not believe in.

A Learning Lab for Love

One time I heard Brother Guy Consolmagno, a Jesuit monastic who is the director of the Vatican Observatory,* give an excellent talk about science and theology. Brother Guy said that no scientist ever imagines they have reached the end, discovered all there is to know

---

* Betcha didn't know the Vatican has one of the world's best observatories. Neither did I, till Brother Guy told us. Brother Guy also told us, trying not to blush under his beard, that the Vatican Observatory employs some of the world's best astronomers, including himself.

in their field. Rather, the scientist imagines that they are one in a long line of wonderers, theorizers, testers, discoverers, and reporters. All each scientist hopes to do is correct, ever so slightly, the course of all the science that came before them, perhaps just by nudging the field a degree or two this way or that, so that the next generation of scientists will be aimed a little more directly at the truth.

Theology, he said, is the same. We ought not imagine we know everything there is to know about God, or even if we did, that we would know how to live according to that knowledge. Rather, every theologian stands in a long line of theologians, offering (in cooperation with the Spirit of the living Christ) small correctives to the course of theology up to now, extending to the next generation of theologians an ever so slightly more accurate directionality for future wonderings. There's a boldness in trusting oneself to find out something that wasn't known before—and a humility in it, at the exact same time, knowing that those who come next will doubtless correct your mistakes or see more clearly what was occluded from your sight.

I would add, then, to Brother Guy's exposition, that the church is like that too. Or at least it could be. In this imagining, the church is full of Christian or Christ-curious people who are exploring together, wondering and discerning together, trying and failing and trying again together, concerning the project of wanting to want what God wants. They know other people have tried this before: the stories of our ancestors in faith are entrusted to us in the Bible, stories of failure and success, stories of hope and heartache. And since the canon's closure, many more generations of devoted disciples have dedicated their lives to a long obedience in the same direction.[*]

---

[*] Yeah, like Eugene Peterson's classic *A Long Obedience in the Same Direction* (1980), except there he's describing the individual life of Christian discipleship, and here we're talking about a communal project.

The church, then, is far from the place where we gather to confirm the rightness of everything we already know about God, the universe, and everything. Instead, it's a place where we come to report what we've discovered about this world God still loves, and to describe the sticky wickets that have us tied in theological knots, and to ask for help getting unstuck. We celebrate each other's findings, mourn each other's disappointments, and challenge each other's misunderstandings (willful or accidental). We help each other do this life of faith better, all of us together incrementally course-correcting all the time, aiming more and more true at the heart of God all the time.

In *A New Kind of Christianity* (2010), Brian McLaren asked, "What do we do about the church?" He opined that the North American, mostly white, Protestant church of which he is a doctor* would need significant renovation to nurture the church's people in their Christian faith in seasons to come. It would be difficult but not complicated, he said, because the church in every age is intended to be, before (and perhaps even instead of) anything else, a school for love.

"The still more excellent way" of love (1 Cor. 12:31b) is "the one grand calling," McLaren says (171); we're only meant to figure out the curriculum, the governance, the liturgy, the relationships, the whole set of practices that would turn the church into a "Jesus dojo," which is McLaren quoting our mutual friend Mark Scandrette**— meaning that here, gathered together, the church would apply itself to learning more and more and more about how to embody the love that Jesus said was the beginning, middle, and end of everything God wants from and for us.***

---

* "Doctor of the church" is a title formally bestowed by the Roman Catholic Church on scholars and saints who have contributed significantly to the church's understanding of itself through their writing. I'm borrowing it for Brian because, well, what else is he?

** In *Soul Graffiti* (2008).

*** Mark 12:28–34, e.g.

It concerns me a little that Galileo Church might accidentally promote the idea that Christian faith, or the Christian ethic of love as the practice of faith, or even justice as love in public, are things that can be learned as matters of cognitive contemplation. I (and lots of other Galileo people) grew up in a strain of Christianity that promoted as of first importance the understanding of right doctrine, the proof-texted Jenga tower blocks to which I had to give my intellectual assent as the content of my faith. It's not only the Jenga tower we're hoping *not* to replicate at Galileo Church; it's the whole idea that Christianity is an analytical pursuit that we have to *think* about correctly.*

McLaren helps us narrow the school metaphor a bit, zipping through the locker-lined hallways till we get to the chem lab, where students in borrowed safety goggles sit on stools, light their Bunsen burners, follow the directions of their ancestors in chemistry, and try to make something cool happen. Or maybe it's a language lab, where learners sit in cubicles with giant headphones on, shaping their mouths in all new ways to speak a language their tongues and hearts don't yet know. Or maybe it's Brother Guy's observatory, a star lab where mathematicians take turns measuring streaks of light in the distant sky; or a biology lab where experimenters excitedly show each other the microdiscovery they've made through the refracted lenses of a microscope; or an art studio where there's ample encouragement and plentiful paint for everyone's attempt to make something beautiful and true.

Labs, I'm saying, are the places where learning happens by application, by trying out in practice what you've read or wondered

---

* I am absolutely down with thinking hard and thinking well and thinking honestly about the Christian faith. But if that's what church is, if that's all it is, or primarily what it is—a think tank for Jesus's followers to think more and think rightly about God, the universe, and everything—I'm thinking that's not going to yield very much more of what God actually wants. I should also say, that's not at all what McLaren is pushing for—church as think tank, that is.

about; where the wonderings of the mind can be embodied, materialized, seen and heard and touched; where the Word of God puts on flesh, the Logic of God becomes human.

Could the church be a learning lab for love? Not just talking about love, or wishing for more love in the world, or scheduling an outpouring of love through our rotations at the community food pantry . . . but actually trying it out, trying to actually love each other by seeing each other, and letting other people see us, so clearly that we can tell when the other person is depressed or anxious or having an MS flare or flourishing in their new job?

If the church could be a learning lab for love, we would build in the possibility—nay, the certainty—that sometimes we're going to try something that doesn't work. I'm going to be too frank when what you needed in the moment was some softness, some swaddling; you're going to say yes when you really should've said no and then fret about how to get out of it; we're going to cross the gossip line when we started with such a good intention to enlist other people's sympathy for someone we all care about. It's a lab. We don't expect everything we try in here to *work*. We employ some safety mechanisms to keep us from causing big explosions and burning the place down, and then we are bold in our attempts.

Friendship as an Outcome

Writing as I am today, on (literally!) the twenty-ninth Sunday of #Coronatide, with no clear end in sight to our socially distanced, shelter-in-place, online-only misery, I am thinking of a lab experiment that Galileo Church had been running continuously for almost seven years before we all went home to work and worship through our screens. We say, among several missional priorities that define the shape of our life together, that we "do real relationship, no bullshit, ever." It's an aspirational pledge to the integration I wrote about before, one that invites and requires us to bring our whole selves into the church, no part of our true human being left outside or covered up.

In the early years of our learning lab, we built plenty of infrastructure to make that "real relationship" pledge possible. We have a robust network of small groups and a gifted spiritual care team that watches over and nurtures their formation. When we're not in the middle of a global pandemic, we eat dinner together and throw parties together and crochet together. In worship we make sure nobody sits alone unless they want to, or takes communion alone unless they need to. We recognize that sometimes the best way to love someone is to give them space and safety to be still and quiet and off to the side but still here with the whole church, and we've built spaces into our Big Red Barn that ensure that possibility. *

When the rogue wave of COVID-19 crashed over us, almost all our infrastructure washed out to sea. No, not the physical structure of the Big Red Barn, thanks be to God. ** But all the programming we had worked so hard on, all the ways we knew how to connect with each other and share our lives and *love* each other, were gone, just like that.

What we had to figure out was, in the absence of church programming—meaning, if we couldn't in good conscience create an increased risk of contagion for each other and for the whole human family by calling large groups of people to gather indoors for an extended period of time to talk and laugh and sing and

---

* At the back of our worship space, there's a small room furnished with fluffy sofas (and a chaise lounge), blankets, coloring books, and earplugs. It's literally called The Quiet Room, and Sunday nights in the Big Red Barn always include an invitation for anyone to hang out in there, adjacent to the worshipping community but not pressed into participation in it. It's part of our fulfillment of another missional priority, to "do kindness around mental illness and mental health, and celebrate neurodiversity."

** Though one big-ass windstorm while we're gathered for worship one Sunday night, and we are toast. *Those* walls are gonna come a-tumblin' down, and it won't be pretty. I'm joking. Sort of.

share food (which is basically church, right?)—*then were we still friends?* Would relationships grown on the scaffolding the church had provided with all those Doodle polls and Facebook events and SignUpGenius forms endure? *Did we know how to love each other*, if the Galileo calendar wasn't full of activities to prop us up and gather us together? Had our learning lab for love yielded good fruit, to mix the metaphor miserably, but you know what I mean?

You can bet I wouldn't be asking that question on the pages of a book I'm reasonably hopeful will be published if the answer weren't "Yeah, thanks be to God." But you would see right through me if I didn't confess that it wasn't easy. It's a vestige, I suppose, of the condescending church, the ecclesial structures and practices that have tricked us into thinking that our participation in church life was always the end goal—like what God needs more of in this world God still loves is more people to go to church more. God does not.

And of course, learning how to love each other in our church-as-school-slash-lab-for-love is meant to make us better and better at loving everybody else too. Beloveds, neighbors, strangers, enemies—loving them, *really* loving them, is the work of a lifetime, a long obedience in the same direction, incremental course corrections that aim us truer day after day, season after season. Church could be (should be?) the place where you're helping me love my conspiracy theory–affirming relatives better, and I'm helping you love your LGBTQ+ nonaffirming parents better, because in here we're testing all the truth-telling, grace-giving, compassion-receiving, identity-honoring *oneness* we can stand. And we're reminding each other to keep our safety goggles on and the fire extinguishers handy, in case of explosions. They happen sometimes—this is real life!—but so far, we haven't burned anything down. Thanks be to God.

14

THE GOSPEL PARA JODER

Back in the day when bulletin boards were a thing—like, a physical cork board for posting announcements and photos, hung in church hallways where folx lingered with their Styrofoam cups of coffee (back in the day when Styrofoam was a thing), scanning for information about what had just happened and what was going to happen next—I got into some trouble for a bulletin board gone wrong. I had read somewhere an old Yiddish proverb:* "God is an earthquake, not an uncle."

In my own young adult life, it was seeming true—that God does not settle me down but instead shakes me up—and I was beginning to rejoice in the freedom of the shake-up, unshackled from the stifling "There, there" of the pacifying "Uncle" God of my childhood. For one thing, I had a job. As a minister. In a church. As a *woman*. God the Earthquake had shaken my spirit loose, thanks be to God! So I cut out big construction-paper letters to staple the sentiment to the bulletin board in the church hallway, thinking some of my church friends would resonate with the God-as-Earthquake experience and take delight in the poetic expression of such.

They did not.

---

* I can't verify that the proverb is Yiddish. It could very well be one of those "preacher stories" that Christian pulpiteers pass along without provenance until we've imagined a backstory that makes it seem more compelling. I dunno.

Or rather, they understood very well that life is plagued with earthquakes that upend everything you thought you knew for sure; they just did not feel safe attributing all that teeth-rattling, bone-jarring, wall-tumbling violence to the kind and gentle God they had come to depend on. What they needed, what they actually came to church for, some of them told me in no uncertain terms, was more certainty, not less. More settling down, less shaking up. More uncle, less earthquake. The bulletin board proverb had to come down. *

Crucified, Resurrected Jesus and the One-Finger Salute

Today, almost three decades later, between my home and the Big Red Barn where Galileo Church meets, I drive by a billboard that says, "Anxious? Jesus brings stability." There's a number to call, or a website to visit; I can't ever remember to check because I fixate on that firm declaration that I have experienced as mostly always ever false. Jesus, in my experience, is inherently *de*stabilizing.

Even when he's calming the storm, hollering, "Peace! Be still!" to the wind and waves, his best friends are terrified, ** because *who does that?* And because he's called them away from their homes and jobs with no discernible plan for success or even survival; and because he prefers to hang out on the murky margins of respectable society, apparently enjoying his downward mobility; and because he deliberately pokes at conventional religious doctrine, morality, and practice, even when he knows it's dangerous; and because he doesn't seem to be subject to the laws of physics—yeah, he's scary AF. More like an earthquake than an uncle, wouldn't you say? De-

---

* See also "24 Frames" by Jason Isbell, definitely not Yiddish but also really good: "You thought God was an architect, now you know / He's something like a pipe bomb ready to blow / And everything you built that's all for show goes up in flames / In twenty-four frames."

** Luke 8:22–25.

stabilizing, and destabilized enough that his family of origin tried to have him committed involuntarily, or the first-century equivalent of such.*

Think of it this way: if Jesus brought stability, if Jesus were more like your favorite, quirky-but-not-crazy uncle, nobody would have wanted to kill him. Not the VRPs (Very Religious Persons), who saw their vocation as stabilization, keeping the people of God carefully aligned with traditional religious practice *and* in quiet cooperation with the imperial powers that were—a difficult needle to thread, indeed, requiring an exquisitely steady hand, making Jesus's boat rocking (an ironic metaphor, in comparison to all his sea stilling and water walking) quite problematic.

Neither would the Roman Empire have exercised its death sentencing prerogative if Jesus had played nicely with the Pax Romana, a tenuous societal stability in which the conqueror produced "peace" by colonizing expansion and maintained "peace" by economic domination and the threat of violence. Jesus, by stirring up a sliver of spiritual unrest among his occupied kindred, and then refusing to acquiesce to the emperor's threats (communicated by lesser officials sworn to protect the Pax by any violence necessary), squared off against Caesar's so-called lordship while under trial in Caesar's so-called justice system. "You can have your taxes," he had been heard to say, "but you can't have *me*."**

And when the empire, thinking to restore the stability Jesus's campaign through the countryside had shaken, sentenced him to death, everybody, even his best friends, thought the old order had been restored. The only certainties in life, right? Death and taxes—and the empire had a lock on both of them.

Matthew is the only gospeler whose passion narrative says anything about earthquakes, and his internal Richter scale clocked two

---

* Mark 3:21.
** Matt. 22:21.

of them. The first: when Jesus took his last breath on Friday afternoon (Matt. 27:50-51). The earth-shattering consequence of his extinguishment, his quiet submission to the power of Death, was itself terrifying, yes? For most of his friends, those who thought they might follow him to the ends of the earth, it was a bridge too far. He was not supposed to *lose*. No messiah worth hitching your wagon to would capitulate so completely, and so *quickly*.

The second: when the women came to the tomb on Sunday morning (Matt. 28:1-2). Somehow, it was equally tectonically unsettling: death working backward in the predawn darkness, the impossibility of an empty tomb for those who had seen with their own eyes where they laid the dead body, the absolute earthquake of resurrection! Behold Jesus striding out of his grave, a smart-ass grin on his face, both arms extended, middle fingers raised in a triumphant (but pacifist!) gesture of defiance toward the systems that thought they had him beat. All day Friday he never said a mumblin' word; like a lamb, he was silent before his shearer. But on Sunday, watch out, world. Death cannot keep its prey. He's *back*, birches.*
The earth shakes, because of course it does.

That last paragraph is where I might have lost you, I know. Because it's *unsettling* for Jesus to flip the bird at anyone, even at Caesar's military-industrial complex, or the VRPs' stifling insistence on religious conformity, or the friends whose ambitions he disappointed, or even Death itself. But if you can make your mind go there for just a second, I'm gambling that it'll feel deeply satisfying to a part of your spirit that gentle Jesus, meek and mild, has never touched.**

---

* Trying to stick with "birches" rather than the sexist but oh-so-satisfying nomenclature it replaces. Help me, Lord. H/t Rebecca Anderson and Gilead Chicago.

** The feeling I'm going for here is the one you experience when someone you love gets a cancer diagnosis, and girds up their loins to face a painful, protracted treatment. They post a photo of themself on Facebook at their third chemo infusion (when they know exactly how much it will hurt, how sick they will

And if you can hold that image, the one of Jesus, whose death and resurrection *each* rattled the very foundations of the earth, giving the postentombment one-finger salute to the powers and principalities, then you can start to appreciate the wonders of the gospel *para joder*.

The Gospel Para Joder

Miguel A. De La Torre, a Cuban-born American Christian social ethicist, introduced the world to an "ethics *para joder*," a concept for which I am truly grateful even as I understand I am not the intended audience for its celebration.* *Joder* is a crude word in Spanish, equivalent to "fuck" in English, and De La Torre uses it to describe a way of comporting oneself in the world that screws with (messes with, fucks with) the powers that be, the systems of oppression that keep poor people poor by ignoring or worsening their suffering. We might rather say an ethics that "undermines" systemic oppression, or that "subverts" the status quo, but De La Torre says "*para joder*," "fucks with," and I'm good with that.

---

feel) with a brave smile and a new T-shirt: "Fuck cancer!" And you would give that photo and that T-shirt one hundred hearts if you could, because that defiance is probably exactly what it takes for your beloved to mentally survive what their body may not.

* See especially De La Torre's *Embracing Hopelessness* (2017), where he prosecutes an argument I don't love but cannot ignore: that "hope" is a component of middle-class, white privilege, wielded to keep the world's poor complacently subjugated (and ourselves conveniently blameless). I'm hoping it's fair to learn from his important course correction to a Christian theology of hope that is beholden to whiteness and wealth, without adopting his rejection of the Christian virtue of hope. His indictment of God for God's inaction on behalf of the oppressed is quite fair but does not give adequate consideration to God's self-limitation for the sake of true partnership with us, God's people, which would mean *we* are coresponsible, at least, for the continued suffering of the poor. "Hope" employed as a "farther along we'll know all about it" pacifier to disorganize and disempower the earth's poor is not Christian hope at all, I'd argue.

Here we are, in this age of institutional decline, including the North American church's decline, each of us left mostly alone to navigate our lives. Here we are at the exact same time under the exponentially increasing demands of social media for our real life – sacrificing participation as a means to feed the insatiable appetite of monstrous market capitalism. Here we are, in yet another age of empire, pressed to maintain social order for the sake of a system that takes our labor and threatens violence, even executes violence more often than we like to think, if not against us then against our neighbors, locally and globally, daring us to do anything about it other than shake our heads and our fists.

The gospel *para joder* is the only gospel that gets any traction here, see? What is necessary in our age is the same as in Jesus's age: a gospel that refuses to submit and support, a gospel that instead subverts and supplants.

And what I am saying is, the church at its best is the locus for learning to fuck with the powers. Like this:

By resting.

The church has no business filling up people's calendars with meetings for prayer and study and worship and service and friendship in a weird, if subconscious, competition to demonstrate that its members are more loyal to the church than to their jobs, or their kids' soccer leagues, or the NFL. The church has no business coercing people into "volunteering" for stuff that weighs down the already-burdened people of God. The church's pastors have no business boasting, in the rhetoric of passive-aggressive complaint, how very busy they have been and are now and ever will be, world without end, amen, amen.*

---

* I have been so guilty of this sin, believing my worth to be measured by my (publicized) exhaustion. I repent. I am forgiven. I try again.

How can the church's people, instead, help each other honor the Sabbath, thus relearning the lesson of our ancestors in the wilderness, newly liberated from Pharaoh's treadmill, acclimating to God's gracious economy? How can the church's pastoral staff and lay leadership model restful rhythms and the boundaries necessary to protect those rhythms? How can we adjust our communal calendar, arrange our communal space, and articulate communal expectations so as to normalize good sleep, energizing naps, joyful recreation, and occasional disengagement from the community for Sabbath's sake?

What if, when the church's people were in need of a nap or a private bathroom or a place to sit quietly for study or prayer or nothing, they could step off the day's treadmill at their place of worship, where comfy couches and fluffy blankets are always available? What if, when people talked about us, they said, "That is one well-rested church!" *Para joder*, indeed.*

By the eucharistic economy.

Various churches have various modes of eucharistic practice. Perhaps a priest blesses the meal with graceful choreography of patens, chalices, napkins; perhaps a layperson cobbles together an extemporaneous prayer over trays of crackers and teensy plastic cups. Perhaps worshippers come to the front to receive the gift one at a time; perhaps trays are passed through the rows. In one place it's flavorless wafers stamped with a cross; in another it's matzo or naan

---

* For this insight I am deeply indebted to Walter Brueggemann's brilliant little book *Sabbath as Resistance: Saying No to the Culture of Now* (2014). And I am in awe of (and support financially) Tricia Hersey's activism through *The Nap Ministry*, wherein she embodies, encourages, and exhorts resistance to the grind and reparations for Black bodies by resting her own Black body, and by installing and photographing public nap-ins as her own politics *para joder*. It surely feels like gospel to me. You can find Hersey's work on Instagram, @thenapministry.

or piecrust or—everybody's favorite—Hawaiian rolls. Grape juice for some; red wine for others. For some it comes around once a quarter, or once a month; at Galileo Church we gather at the Lord's table every Sunday of the world, and talk about all the nonsacramental eating we do together as eucharistic too.

The one consistent thing about the Eucharist from church to church—other than the presence of God in it, whatever the nuances of each church's understanding of that—is that at the Lord's table, there is always *enough*. Enough bread, enough Welch's, and enough mercy to go around. Eucharistic practice absolutely disallows the allotment of more or less to certain people for certain reasons, * and in my denominational heritage the table is truly open to all so that no one is ever turned away. (Jesus ate and drank with everybody, even his enemies, so we figure we should too.)

In *Evangelism After Christendom: The Theology and Practice of Christian Witness* (2007), Bryan Stone explicates the claim that "eucharistic practice is the central ritual of the church's economics" (199). That is to say, when we share the Lord's Supper in memory of Jesus and in anticipation of the reign of God, we are embodying and rehearsing an economic commitment. We are practicing an economics *para joder* (though that's not the language Stone would use, that I know of).

In the alternative economy of the Eucharist, you bring nothing but get everything, trusting God as the giver. Communion becomes a demonstration of the radical sufficiency of God's provision. And because every worshipper approaches the table with empty hands, fully expectant that they, too, will be granted a portion of God's gift, communion is also a demonstration of the radical equity of God's provision. This, says Stone, is the eucharistic economy: sufficiency

---

* See 1 Corinthians 11:17–22, where Paul chides a church for letting some people eat and drink too much while other people don't get any at all, thus preserving the economic hierarchy that our baptisms are meant to flatten.

and equity rehearsed in the ritual meal, and lived out in the more literally economic practices of the church.

So, for example, a eucharistic church ought not build up a fat bank account to protect and preserve its own institutional life while people within it, or people near to it, or people anywhere, are barely getting by. The church ought not spend its money except to do more of the ministry Jesus did with his own body, if the church is to be Christ's body now.* The church ought not clench its own fists tightly around what it's got but instead should practice an open-handed release of resources, sharing all that it has been given.

In this way, the church models for the persons within it that while capitalism will always want us on our knees, trading hours of our wild and precious lives for another cup of specialty coffee or another bottle of trendy beer, we practice our own liberation by an economic practice *para joder*—by wanting less, buying less, spending less, keeping less, and working less.

One sure way Galileo Church knows to keep less is to give more. So in our sixth year we used congregational funds to match financial gifts to an emergency shelter for trans refugees awaiting US asylum in Ciudad Juárez, exercising our co-conspirators' generosity muscle in a way that could not be mistaken as self-interested for the church's sake. In our seventh year we matched financial gifts designated for a sister church in Dallas, one a little newer and founded on a lot less privilege than ours, ultimately writing a check that drained 20 percent of our bank account in one fell swoop, demonstrating our collective trust that God (not Pharaoh) vindicates risk-taking generosity.

---

* Galileo Church's annual spending plan employs these categories: Announcing the Reign of God and Inviting People In; Preaching and Teaching; Healing and Shepherding; Worship and Spirituality; Eating and Drinking with Friends; Calling and Sending; and Welcoming Children. These constituted the ministry of Jesus when he had hands and feet of his own; now he has ours. You can see the church's finance plan at galileochurch.org, under "Conspire With Us."

During the spring and summer of #Coronatide, as of this writing, we have given away block grants of $250 totaling well over $10,000 to any among Galileo's wide circle of co-conspiracy, friendship, and acquaintance who lost gigs or shifts or tips or jobs due to the virus and the slow-moving economic crisis we are still enduring. We do not employ a means test or have any forms to fill out. We just give, kinda recklessly, like a profligate farmer sowing seed indiscriminately, like a prodigal parent welcoming their big spender home.

What if the eucharistic church found ways to do church on the cheap, so it wasn't always pressing people already skeptical of institutional maintenance to give more and more? And what if its people were then free to practice tithing as resistance, a subversive theological practice, a big middle finger to The Man, where The Man is capitalism and its relentless demands on your energies, because every dollar you give away is a dollar The Man can't have? That's the gospel *para joder*, right there.

By our stubborn, baptized existence.

The church that is Christ's body just won't stay dead. The church made up of queer and queer-adjacent spiritual refugees who held on to faith or something like it by their ragged fingernails when everyone around them said God couldn't love them, the church that cheerfully flies its various Pride flags in an otherwise dingy worship space, can't be killed. The church that endures hate mail, and evictions from rented worship spaces, and misery-making mistakes born of our own inexperience, and all the regular, petty meanness that ensues when tensions are high and emotional resources are few—that church, just by existing, is a church *para joder*.

It's something we learned from the LGBTQ+ community, something the LGBTQ+ community learned from communities of resistance that came before them: that *existence* is resistance if your existence is a threat to people's comfort or to the powers' status quo. Every day that you wake up, you fabulous rainbow-colored glitterati unicorn, every day that you dress yourself in the clothes you love most and get out there in the world God still loves, you are a one-person protest. There are people and institutions that wish you would disappear by blending in. Every day that you don't, you inch a little bit closer to the reign o'God.

So it goes for the church that ought not to exist, the church with a big gay sign on its roof, visible from the interstate, inviting people to visit our website and peruse our missional priorities—a very quick test for (in)compatibility and (dis)comfort level. We keep not making safe choices; we keep not taking the easy way out; we keep not being quiet or invisible or keeping things on the down low. We're out, and proud, and *baptized so hard*—meaning, we take our baptized identity, our oneness in Christ, the leveling out of inequity, our genuine appreciation for the quirky, queer gifts we each bring, our various empowerments by the Spirit of the living Christ for the good of the world God still loves, *very* seriously.

What if, when our name came up in conversation around town, people said, "Oh, *that* church? You mean they still exist? Huh. I wouldn't've thought . . ." What if every Sunday of the world, we said the final "Amen!" and walked out of the dimly lit Big Red Barn into the bright afternoon sun like we'd just been resurrected again from the tombs of despair and denigration, all of us together raised again to new life in Christ, every single one of us grinning from ear to ear and flipping the bird (peacefully!) to every person and every power that ever wished otherwise for us? What if the church existed *para joder*?

CONCLUSION

WHAT DO YOU WANT?

Jesus knew they talked about him behind his back, the VRPs, the ones who imagined that religion is about restriction—knowing who and what to say no to, the substance of devout belief and practice. He knew they said his habit of saying yes to every dinner invitation was his Achilles' heel. He knew they strategized ways to catch him with his theological pants down, hoping to embarrass him by making public his scandalous inattention to religiously restrictive details.

He called them out on it sometimes with a disarming-by-laughing-it-off strategy, saying out loud in front of a crowd what they had only whispered to each other:

> "The Son of [Humanity] has come eating and drinking, and you say, 'Look, a glutton and a drunkard, a friend of tax collectors and sinners!'" (Luke 7:34)

It seems his detractors had been focus-grouping a potential charge they hoped would discredit him in the eyes of his fans. "A glutton and a drunkard" echoes the language of Deuteronomy 21:18–21, where our ancestors in faith outlined a process for ridding the world of stubborn and rebellious sons. If a young man's parents had had it up to *here* with their boy's disobedience, they could recommend his stoning to death in the public square, as long as their neighbors could confirm the charges of gluttony and drunkenness. Harsh? Yes. A kind of wishful threat-making many parents have succumbed to on their worst parenting day ever? Sure.

Who Wouldn't Want a Messiah Like That?

I think Jesus understood something the VRPs didn't, though. I think he knew that people, all kinds of people, really love life and always want more of it. I think that as the Humanest Human, the Son of Humanity, one of the best things Jesus learned about us is that we are all of us "gluttons and drunkards." That is to say, when we're feeling healthy and strong in our minds and spirits, life is a sticky-ripe peach dangling from a branch bent with fruit and buzzy with wasps on a glorious summer day, plucked and handed to us by someone who loves us dearly, someone who waits with delight to see our eyes widen as peach juice runs down our chin and the glands in the back of our mouth constrict with the sour sweetness. That is to say, when we humans are at our best, we always want *more*.

They said he ate too much, and drank too much, and with all the wrong people. I say, "Who *wouldn't* want a messiah like that?" Who wouldn't want a messiah who invites himself over for dinner, and brings some of his own guests along, and starts acting like the host as soon as he gets there, and wonders "if you could just pass that hummus, those olives, that cheese, over this way one more time? And is there any wine left in that bottle? Hmm, well, let's see if I can't do something about that. Hang on a sec. Y'all got any of those big water jars? The really big ones?" Seriously—who wouldn't go with a guy like that, if he asked you to walk this way, to come and see? This guy, with peach juice dribbling down his beard while he savors every single sublime bite?

Well. Some people wouldn't. But plenty of spiritual refugees would, so many of them that his bad reputation would start to include his fraternization with the likes of them—the so-called sinners and the despised tax collectors, all the ones kept on the outside of the bounds of respectability, thrown out or left out, put down and talked about the same way he was. And that's the other thing he understood about us: that the ones who've got no reputation left to protect are the ones who throw the best parties. Guaranteed.

For Jesus, who "came eating and drinking," casting his lot with the cast-outs and the castaways, the reign of God meant taking every chance he could to say yes. Yes to healing and health, even on the Sabbath. Yes to unbinding people from whatever had ahold of them, even if it felt dangerous. Yes to releasing people from shame and guilt, yes to restoring "daughters" and "sons" to beloved status in the family of God. Yes to anybody who argued convincingly against his initial "no." Yes to dinner at your house, or mine, even and especially if we were, umm, questionable dinner companions. He was like us, and more so, the Humanest Human, always wanting more of this amazing life in this world God still loves.

On the Other End of the Rope

Christianity, as it turns out, doesn't start and end with what we understand about God, the universe, and everything, nor is it only or even mostly about what we believe about all those things. It's also not in the first place about what we do, how we behave, the careful restrictiveness of religious observance.

It's about what we *want*. It's about wanting what God wants, and wanting that more and more and more, until life feels abundant and eternal and delicious and drunken with possibility—the possibility that God could, right this very minute, be showing our grandmas who are at home in God's heart how to find their place at a banquet table stacked with a meal they didn't have to cook and won't have to clean up after, where they will sit in joyful shalom alongside their beloveds and their former enemies and all the ones they were afraid of. It's about the end of violence and coercion by weapon and speech. It's about the elevation of the small and the stepped on, and about privilege tending toward zero in the equitable accounting of God's math. It's about every lonely heart finding companionship. It's about the earth itself returned to flourishing, flowering, flowing with God's intended very-goodness. It's about systems of oppression tumbling into the sea in a baptism that never lets us go.

It's about wanting more of that, not only someday but *now*, not only in the heart of God but *here*. It's about wanting that so badly you dream about it. Write songs about it. March in the streets for it. Whisper prayers into the air for it. Get with your friends every seven days or so to talk about it and eat and drink in anticipation of it, whetting your appetite for more of it, even while the peach juice runs down your chin. Always more. We never get enough. We always want more of what God wants. *

"The church in the power of the Spirit is not yet the [reign] of God, but it is its anticipation in history," said one of the church's doctors. ** In my mind's eye I see the church's people, some of us all the way Christian today, some of us mostly not but still here, all of us wearing serious shoes for serious work, our heels dug into the mud of this world God still loves. We are clutching in our rough, calloused hands (we've been doing this awhile) a rope, taut with tension, leaning back with all our weight, flexing our quads and

---

* For more about Christianity as *desire*, see especially James K. A. Smith's *Desiring the Kingdom: Worship, Worldview, and Cultural Formation* (2009). So, so good. Or try Ellen Davis's Westminster Bible Companion commentary on Proverbs, Ecclesiastes, and Song of Songs (2000). In the section on the Song, Davis appreciates the unconsummated love of the lovers who just keep *wanting* each other excruciatingly for eight chapters. She argues convincingly that this is (also) the experience of the human heart seeking God's heart—we're always wanting, never quite getting there, but it's the *wanting* that really matters. Which is why, she says, the Song is "wisdom literature." I believe her.

** Jürgen Moltmann, in *The Church in the Power of the Spirit* (1993), 196. Or, y'know, the whole book.

glutes as we grunt and sweat. Sometimes we laugh when one of us loses their balance and sits down hard in the mud; we offer a hand to help them scramble back up. We are pulling together, more or less coordinating our strength, determined in our effort. "Pull! Pull! Pull!" we shout for encouragement. People tap out when they're tired and come back when they're rested. It's ridiculously hard. It's ridiculously fun.

On the other end of the rope? Silly goose, it's the reign of God. It's the justice (love in public) the long arc of the moral universe bends toward. It's everything God wants, and it's all we want, and we want so much more of it, right here, right now. We're gluttons and drunkards for the reign of God. We're sinners and tax collectors, kicked out and kept out, ready to get our hands dirty for the reign of God. We're saying yes because it seems good to the Holy Spirit and to us. We're saying yes because God gets everything God wants; because God has gotten, is getting, will get, *every single thing* God wants, and we just . . . want that.

Don't you?